BRANFORD MARSALIS

Jazz Musician

—PEOPLE TO KNOW—

BRANFORD MARSALIS

Jazz Musician

Bob Bernotas

ENSLOW PUBLISHERS, INC.

Bloy St. and Ramsey Ave.   P.O. Box 38
Box 777   Aldershot
Hillside, N.J. 07205   Hants GU12 6BP
U.S.A.   U.K.

Library of Congress Cataloging-in-Publication Data

Bernotas, Bob.
    Branford Marsalis : jazz musician / Bob Bernotas
        p. cm. — (People to know)
        Discography: p.
        Includes bibliographical references (p.   ) and index.
        ISBN 0-89490-495-7
        1. Marsalis, Branford—Juvenile literature. 2. Jazz musicians—
United States—Biography—Juvenile literature. [1. Marsalis,
Branford. 2. Musicians. 3. Afro-Americans—Biography. 4. Jazz.]
I. Series.
ML3930.M32B47 1994
788.7'165'092—dc20
        [B]   93-47358
                                                        CIP
                                                      AC MN
Printed in the United States of America

10 9 8 7 6 5 4 3 2 1

Illustration Credits:
Courtesy of A & M Records, p. 49; Courtesy of Columbia Records, pp. 44,
61; © David Lee, p. 69; © Enid Farber, pp. 27, 33, 80; © Milton J.
Hinton, p. 19; ©NBC Photo, pp. 6, 10, 89.

Cover Illustration:
© NBC Photo.

Contents

1 *The Tonight Show* 7

2 New Orleans 13

3 "I Didn't Want
To Be A Musician" 21

4 "He's the Leader" 35

5 "I Play What I Like" 46

6 New Doors 56

7 Crazy People Music 66

8 "A Charmed Life" 74

9 "Everything" 86

Chronology 97

Selected Discography 99

Chapter Notes 101

Further Reading 109

Index 110

Branford Marsalis

The Tonight Show

On March 22, 1992, an era in television history ended. After twenty-nine and a half years, Johnny Carson stepped down as the host of *The Tonight Show*, NBC's late-night talk-variety program. Also leaving *The Tonight Show* was Carson's bandleader of twenty-four and a half years, Doc Severinsen.

To replace Carson, NBC chose Jay Leno—a popular stand-up comic who, at the age of forty-two, was twenty-four years younger than the outgoing host. The network hoped that Leno's broad appeal could win back the eighteen- to thirty-five-year-old audience that in recent years had left *The Tonight Show*'s fold. As a key part of this "youth campaign," the show's producers hired a new musical director—thirty-one-year-old saxophonist Branford Marsalis.

Throughout the 1980s, first as a member of his brother Wynton's quintet and then as the leader of his own band, Marsalis built a solid reputation as one of the so-called "young lions" of jazz. During that time he had received seven Grammy Award nominations in the jazz field. But Marsalis' musical interests stretched well beyond the mainstream of jazz. He had toured and recorded with the pop singer Sting, performed in concert with the classic rock and roll band the Grateful Dead, and even acted in a couple of movies.

When Helen Kushnick—then *The Tonight Show's* executive producer—first approached Marsalis, he told her he was not interested in the job, or "gig" as musicians say. "And I thought about it," he recalls, "and I said, yeah, there's a lot of reasons to be interested."[1] So in October 1991 Kushnick, who also is Jay Leno's manager, arranged a meeting between the saxophonist and the comedian. The two immediately hit it off.

"He's incredibly charismatic," Leno notes. "The first time I met the guy, I realized he was somebody who could say in four words what most people took 25 or 30 words to say."[2] Marsalis was offered the job, and he accepted. "Branford was the first choice," the new host told *Down Beat* magazine. "There really was no second choice."[3]

When NBC officially announced Marsalis' hiring the following March, fellow saxophonist David Sanborn proclaimed, "The quality of music on television just went up 200 percent."[4] Certainly, the chance to make music for the largest possible audience was one reason that Marsalis accepted the offer. One writer estimated that by the end of Marsalis' first full year on the show, "he will be seen by more people than have ever seen Miles Davis perform."[5]

As musical director, Marsalis wanted complete creative control over the music that would be played on the show. Leno backed him up and made certain that the network agreed. "He calls all the shots," Leno explains. ". . . He tells me what we're going to hear tonight, which is fine with me."[6]

Since Marsalis took over the *Tonight Show* band, jazz has played a bigger role on the program than ever before. Still he does not see himself as a tele-evangelist for jazz. "We're just spreading the gospel of good music, if we're spreading the gospel at all," Marsalis maintains.[7]

For example, on Leno's May 25, 1992 debut broadcast, Marsalis selected "Nutty"—a tune written by jazz pianist-composer Thelonious Monk—to introduce the members of his band. That same night the band also covered a Led Zeppelin hit. "I'm not trying to bring jazz to the masses," Marsalis admits. "You can't. . . . What you can bring to the masses is a sensibility of good musicianship."[8]

But along with the chance to play good music—and *some* jazz—on television every night, Marsalis had other reasons for taking the *Tonight Show* gig. Ever since he

Throughout early 1992 Marsalis was a key part of NBC's promotional campaign for the revamped *Tonight Show*. Here he appears in a publicity shot with the new host, Jay Leno.

became a professional musician in 1980, Marsalis had spent most of his time on the road, traveling from city to city and country to country on buses and planes, eating in strange restaurants, sleeping in strange hotels. The travel was an exhausting grind, and he welcomed the chance to sit down in one place for a while.

"I'll be stationary," he told the *New York Times* with obvious relief. "I'll wake up in the same bed day after day, something that I haven't done since college."[9]

Being stationary, Marsalis also could devote more time to his musical growth. "I'll be able to practice for the first time in years,"[10] he said. He also looked forward to going back to college, which his nomadic life made next to impossible. "I'm gonna take saxophone lessons at USC," he announced eagerly, "and try to get my history degree."[11] He also planned to study acting.

But one thing Marsalis did not care about was the well-known "glitz and glamour" of Hollywood. He was not after a lifestyle of the rich and famous. He did not want to become one of the "beautiful people." "I'm not thrilled with stardom and fame," he declared with disdain. "Beautiful people don't go to school."[12]

Finally, Marsalis' newfound stability would allow him more time to spend with his son, Reese, who turned seven years old in 1992. This was especially important to him since, after Marsalis and his wife Teresa separated in November 1991, Reese continued to live in New York with his mother. *The Tonight Show's*

Monday-through-Friday taping schedule allows him to head east whenever he wants to spend a weekend with Reese.

Despite his five-year contract with NBC, Marsalis insists that he does not plan to make *The Tonight Show* his permanent home. He's too well-rounded and too restless for that. "Based on all the things that I have on my résumé," he wonders, "what would make anybody think that I would want to do one show for 30 years?"[13]

Wherever he is performing and whatever musical style or setting he is working in, Branford Marsalis always tries to do one thing—to present good music to his audiences. So as long as he is musical director of *The Tonight Show*, he plans to continue that mission. "That's my job," he states bluntly. "Find quality music and introduce a new attitude . . . to the television-viewing public."[14]

New Orleans

New Orleans, Louisiana, often is called "the birthplace of jazz." Starting in the late 1800s and for decades after, the social life of African Americans in this bustling southern port city centered around dozens of clubs and secret societies. Each of these organizations had its own brass band that played for all sorts of occasions—parades, dances, picnics, even funerals. The exciting and vibrant music known as "jazz" grew out of the brass bands of New Orleans.

Naturally a large number of creative jazz musicians have hailed from the so-called "Crescent City"—from the great trumpeter Louis Armstrong, who was born there at the turn of the century, to the Marsalis family of today. Branford Marsalis, the oldest of six brothers, was born in nearby Breaux Bridge—the "Crawfish Capital of the World"—on August 26, 1960.

His father, Ellis Marsalis, is both an accomplished jazz pianist and a respected music educator. Since the 1950s the New Orleans-born musician has worked with both traditional and modern style jazz groups in and around his home town.

In 1974 Ellis Marsalis became head of the music department at the New Orleans Center for the Creative Arts, a school for artistically-oriented students. At that time the family moved from the small Cajun town of Breaux Bridge to that big city at the mouth of the Mississippi River—New Orleans.

Marsalis left the New Orleans school in 1986 to become coordinator of the jazz program at Virginia Commonwealth University in Richmond. Currently he is head of the music department and professor of jazz studies at the University of New Orleans.

Dolores Marsalis, Branford's mother, worked as a singer and a substitute teacher before becoming a full-time homemaker. Her family tree has some deep musical roots of its own. On her father's side she is related to Wellman Braud, who played bass with Duke Ellington's orchestra in the 1920s and 1930s. The legendary New Orleans clarinetist, Alphonse Picou, is a relative on her mother's side.

It is not very surprising, then, that most of the Marsalis children became interested in music. "It was very important for me," Dolores Marsalis has explained, "that they would have some aesthetic thing that they could express themselves through."[1] In time four of the Marsalis sons followed a musical path—Branford plays the saxophone; Wynton, who is fourteen months younger, plays the trumpet; Delfeayo, now in his mid-twenties, doubles as a trombonist and record producer; and Jason, still in his teens, is an emerging drum talent.

Branford's first instrument was the piano, which he began to play at the age of four. Three years later he took up the clarinet so that he could play in the school band. Then at age fifteen, Branford decided to switch to the saxophone. His father got him an alto saxophone, which he believed was the most difficult member of the saxophone family. Still in only six months, Branford was good enough to make the all-state band. "Branford had the most natural ability in music," his mother claims, "no doubt about it."[2]

Music came easily to Branford, but practicing bored him. The following year he "goofed off," and despite his ability, he failed to make all-state. "I'll admit it," he told *Down Beat* magazine. "I'm the classic lazy cat. I didn't want to be bothered; I didn't want to practice. I just wanted to exist."[3]

In that sense Branford was quite different from his younger brother Wynton, with whom he shared a bedroom for seventeen years. Today a well-known jazz trumpeter, Wynton was an Eagle Scout at twelve, soloed with the New Orleans Philharmonic at sixteen, and was a consistent straight-A honor student.

"Wynton was very disciplined," his brother recalls. "He knew when he was 12 that he wanted to be a musician. I just wanted to be an adolescent knucklehead, and I was very good at it."[4] Nevertheless the young Branford was a capable football player and track athlete.

In the mid-1960s Branford, Wynton, and nine other African-American children integrated an otherwise all-white Catholic elementary school. The situation was not easy, and each brother had his own way of dealing with it. Branford always tried to deflect trouble and defuse tense circumstances. Wynton, on the other hand, would be more likely to confront his tormentors head-on.

Despite childhood differences in their personalities and musical tastes—many of which have carried over into their adulthood—the two brothers were close. "He was always my boy," Wynton says of his older brother. ". . . I could always talk to him."[5]

With their father's encouragement the teenaged brothers formed their own funk band called The Creators. Wynton already had been drawn toward jazz, but his older brother's musical tastes were more like those of a typical teen. Branford listened to rock groups such as Pink Floyd and funk bands like Earth, Wind & Fire. "I loved Led Zeppelin—I camped out for tickets in the rain," he recalls. "I dragged Wynton to Parliament/Funkadelic concerts."[6]

Growing up, Branford's favorite saxophonists were fusion players David Sanborn and Grover Washington, Jr. Although their music was often creative and interesting, it did not fit into the mainstream of jazz. "I was a fusionhead," he admits without shame.[7]

In those days Branford thought jazz was "corny." He didn't begin to like the music until he was much older, which—given his background—many people find surprising. "Everybody thinks our family was, 'Oh, let's play jazz for breakfast, jazz for lunch, jazz for dinner,'"[8] he once remarked.

But although Ellis Marsalis never forced his sons into jazz, he certainly did his best to expose them to it. As a teenager Branford would accompany his father to his gigs, although he paid little attention to the music. "But when you grow up in a certain environment," he observes, "there are a lot of things in the air that you pick up."[9]

What Ellis and Dolores Marsalis did insist upon was discipline and achievement. They set high standards for their sons, and expected them to excel in whatever they chose to do. "In our family," Delfeayo Marsalis has noted, "you are either the best or you don't do it. Our parents always instilled in us a certain pride and dignity."[10]

Their mother was especially watchful, Wynton

recalled years later. "I can still hear her voice calling me, 'Wynton, bring your skinny behind in here and practice that trumpet, then do your *homework*.'"[11]

All the Marsalis brothers agree that they benefited from their parents' close attention, even the occasionally undisciplined Branford. Still, Ellis Marsalis downplays the role that he may have had in his sons' success. "All I did," he maintains, "was make sure they had the best so they could be the best; they did the rest."[12]

The Marsalis family has always been a close one. In an article for *TV Guide,* Wynton Marsalis described a typical Christmas celebration in his boyhood home. "The aromas of food would seep through the house and they would heighten my feelings of anticipation,"[13] he remembered, as their mother stayed up late on Christmas eve preparing special dishes for the next day's dinner. The main course—either roast turkey or barbecued chicken and ribs—would be accented by such New Orleans favorites as gumbo, jambalaya, greens, potato salad, corn bread, and fruitcake for desert.

After dinner the four oldest brothers—Branford, Wynton, Ellis III, and Delfeayo—would choose sides for their annual football game. Their father played quarterback for both teams. When the game was over they all would return to the house for the musical portion of the day.

"My brother [Branford] and I would get out our horns," Wynton reminisced, "although back then we

Teenage musicians Wynton and Branford Marsalis practicing in their father's New Orleans classroom.

really couldn't play very well, so usually we just sang while our father played Christmas tunes in a jazz style."[14] Ellis Marsalis and his sons still enjoy performing together.

As they matured the two oldest Marsalis brothers began to explore classical music. "When we were in high school," Branford recalls, "Wynton and I sang all of the Bach chorales—he sang the melody while I sang the bass part."[15] By that time the teenaged Wynton already was a fairly accomplished classical trumpeter. As adults both brothers have recorded classical albums.

Branford graduated high school in 1978 and enrolled in Southern University, a predominantly black college located in Louisiana's capital city of Baton Rouge. He majored in history, but also studied music with Alvin Batiste, a brilliant jazz clarinetist and a frequent collaborator with Ellis Marsalis.

Batiste was impressed with the young saxophonist's ability, but he felt that Branford had gone as far as he could at Southern. "Warning" Branford that he would flunk him if he came back for a second year, Batiste convinced him to transfer to the Berklee College of Music in Boston, Massachusetts. In Berklee's more intensive musical environment, Batiste believed, Branford would be able to develop his talent to its fullest.

"I Didn't Want
To Be A Musician"

"Music was always there," Branford Marsalis once told *New York* magazine, "but I didn't want to be a musician. I wanted to be a lawyer but flunked a big class; wanted to play football but blew out my knee; wanted to go into history but lost interest. Those doors closed one by one until the only door left open was music."[1]

So nearly out of options, Marsalis arrived at the Berklee College of Music in the fall of 1979 and decided to apply himself to the study of music. "I went there," he has explained, "with a specific thing in mind: experiment, meet musicians, practice, get down to New York. . . . I didn't just show up and say, 'Teach me.' "[2]

Berklee, he soon discovered, was overflowing with talented student musicians, all concentrated in a single place. For example, his roommates were saxophonist

Donald Harrison, a New Orleans friend who also transferred from Southern University, and drummer Marvin "Smitty" Smith. Today these men are two of the top players in jazz. And just down the hall lived Jeff "Tain" Watts, who now is the drummer in Marsalis' band.

At Southern, Marsalis was at the head of the class. But at Berklee, he would have to work hard in order to survive in the competitive and challenging environment. "Suddenly," he notes, "I was at the bottom of the totem pole and it was either stay mediocre or practice and improve."[3]

Marsalis practiced and he did improve. He also gained valuable experience while earning his rent money by playing in all sorts of bands in the Boston area. He even played the clarinet at bar mitzvahs. In fact he played everything but jazz.

Finally at age nineteen, Marsalis began to feel drawn toward jazz. He remembered a record that his father first played for him when he was fourteen years old. Titled *Bird with Strings,* it featured Charlie Parker, the great and influential jazz saxophonist of the 1940s and early 1950s. At that time the young Branford preferred the fusion players. But even then he understood that Parker's music belonged on a different and higher level.

"I realized that if I was ever gonna seriously deal with the saxophone," Marsalis recalls, "listening to the guys that I was listening to was never gonna get me there like *that* record was gonna get me there." Five more years passed before he really started to take jazz seriously. Nevertheless that moment, he maintains, "was the turning point for me."[4]

He knew that he had a lot to learn. Jazz is a complex and subtle music. It requires a strong technical foundation and the ability to improvise, to create spontaneous melodies that make musical sense. It also takes a great deal of study and practice, Marsalis discovered, to master this music. "Jazz music is like baseball . . . ," he has observed. "There are all these little things that take years to learn how to do."[5]

But even though he had begun to examine this music more closely, Marsalis still did not expect to have a career in jazz. Then in the summer of 1980, his brother Wynton went on tour with drummer Art Blakey and his group, the Jazz Messengers. (Wynton was on vacation from New York City's renowned Julliard School where he was studying music.) When the band performed in Boston, naturally, Branford was in the audience.

He was thrilled to see his younger brother on stage, and it inspired him. "I was so proud, so happy," Branford remembers, "When I saw him I got fired up and thought, 'Man, I want to do this, too.' "[6] He told Wynton that he really was going to practice. Now he knew that he wanted to be a professional musician.

Wynton, at first, was not convinced. He remembered

how, as a talented teenager, Branford would rather have done anything than practice the saxophone. But Branford meant what he said. "For the next six months," he explains, "I jumped in and started practicing. I even stopped watching television and buying pop records. I must have bought two hundred to three hundred jazz records during that period."[7]

Branford progressed quickly. Later that same summer Art Blakey formed a ten-piece band for a European tour and hired Marsalis to play baritone saxophone (an instrument that at the time was new to him). Now even Wynton, who also was in the band, had to believe that his older brother was serious about jazz.

During that tour Marsalis appeared on his first recording, *Live at Montreux and North Sea,* released on the Timeless label. The album captures Blakey's "little big band" in performance at jazz festivals in Switzerland and the Netherlands. Each summer the European festival circuit makes up an important part of many jazz musicians' schedules.

Returning to Berklee in the fall of 1980, Marsalis continued studying and practicing. He joined other budding talents in the school's practice rooms, where they held frequent jam sessions. Down through the years, jazz musicians have found that the most effective and enjoyable way to sharpen their skills is to do it collectively, by "jamming" with other players.

Although Marsalis enjoyed his musical experiences in

Boston, other aspects of his stay there were not so positive. He was, at first, surprised to find that racial attitudes in this northern city could be as intolerant and bigoted as they were in the South where he grew up.

Once while walking down the street, three white men came up to him and one called him a racist name. The usually restrained Marsalis lost his cool and punched the bigot. Then the other two men jumped in. The police arrived and let the three white men go, but they threatened to arrest Marsalis. "They were gonna put me up for assault," he marvels " . . . And I said, 'Oh, so that's Boston.'"[8]

Another time he and two white companions, on their way to a jazz concert, ventured into the tough all-white neighborhood of South Boston. They were confronted by a gang of white teenagers yelling racist slurs and carrying baseball bats. The three decided to make a run for it, but his friends fell behind and were caught by the mob.

Marsalis made it to a gas station and asked for help. "This big [white] dude gets out of a van with a *chain* in his hand," Marsalis recounts. ". . . He says, 'They're [messing] with you 'cause you're black, aren't they? I hate that.' And he went out there with his boy and got my friends." Marsalis was angry and shaken, but had learned a worthwhile lesson. "I can't really indict the whole neighborhood,"[9] he reasoned. After all someone from the area did come to his aid.

During that year's Christmas break, Marsalis landed a two-week gig playing *tenor* saxophone with the big band of vibraphonist Lionel Hampton. It was the first time that he ever played this instrument in a jazz context. Still, Marsalis managed to impress his new boss and ended up with more solos than anyone else in the band—except Hampton himself.

Having spent more than fifty years as a professional musician, the then seventy-two-year-old Hampton was—and still is—one of the most admired jazz veterans. For decades he has had a reputation for hiring young players. Hampton sincerely enjoys giving a boost to emerging jazz talents, such as that eager Berklee student Branford Marsalis.

However, musicians who have worked for him are quick to add that "Hamp" is also a shrewd businessman. He knows that he can pay these youngsters much less than the more established "name" players. Nevertheless many future giants of jazz got their earliest big-time experience with Lionel Hampton's bands.

Marsalis had intended to return to Berklee in January once the gig with Hampton ended. Instead he picked up his alto saxophone and joined another big band, this time led by trumpeter Clark Terry.

From the early 1930s to the mid 1940s, big bands were the principal type of jazz groups. These ensembles consisted of thirteen to seventeen pieces—usually four or five saxophones, three or four trumpets, three or four

Lionel Hampton, jazz legend and master of the vibraphone, gave
Marsalis one of his first big-time gigs in December 1980.

trombones, piano, bass, drums, and often guitar. Many young musicians developed valuable skills, both as soloists and ensemble players, as "sidemen" in the big bands.

By the mid-to-late 1940s, however, the big bands began to die out for three main reasons. First, jazz is a music that is constantly evolving and changing. The new jazz that emerged in the mid-1940s, known as "bebop," relied more on small combos of four to seven pieces. Their music made most of the larger ensembles seem outdated and old-fashioned.

Second, the big bands spent the majority of their time on the road, playing one-nighters, or if they were lucky, week-long engagements. Leading a big band was always an expensive enterprise, and travel costs were a major part of the band's budget. It became even more expensive when, starting in the mid-1940s, the cost of travel increased.

At the same time many ballrooms, theaters, and nightclubs—the places where big bands played—began to close. With higher expenses and fewer places to work, only a small handful of leaders could afford to maintain a big band on a permanent basis.

And third, during the mid-to-late 1940s American popular music underwent an important change. The big bands were losing their hold on the pop market. Popular singers emerged as the dominant force on the music scene, and the big bands soon fell far behind. As their audience shrank, the number of working bands dwindled drastically. By the mid-1950s rock and roll had pushed big band jazz out of the pop field entirely.

So by the early 1980s, when Branford Marsalis started his career as a professional jazz musician, very few of these valuable "training grounds" still existed. Lionel Hampton was one of the fortunate surviving big band leaders. Most other big bands, such as the Art Blakey and Clark Terry groups that Marsalis worked in, are temporary ensembles, organized to play a particular gig or a relatively short-term tour.

Terry's 1981 group was a collection of top young players, sort of a "college all-star band." Like Marsalis, most of these musicians have gone on to successful careers in jazz, and many of them still keep in touch. Matt Finders, for example, one of Terry's trombonists, now plays in Marsalis' *Tonight Show* band.

For about four months the Clark Terry band toured Europe and the United States. Money was low, and the musicians had to pay their own hotel expenses. Still these players, most of them in their early twenties, were grateful for the experience.

On these trips, first with Blakey and then with Terry, Marsalis learned that life on the road—except when you actually are performing—can be terribly dull. In addition he found that being cooped up with the same people for weeks and months at a time can make the most even-tempered person a little edgy. And so

Marsalis discovered a way to relieve the boredom and tension. He became one of the band's resident practical jokers.

The mischief that Marsalis and his cohorts created was quite harmless. For example, a bandmate, opening the door to his hotel room after a late night out, might find the knob covered with mustard or shaving cream. Or while dressing for the gig, one of the players might discover powdered soap in his shoes. Whenever anyone asked who was responsible for the prank, the answer was always the same. The victims would be told that the culprit was "Darby Hicks"—a fictitious character.

One of Darby Hicks's favorite gags was to rearrange the valves on a trumpet so it would not play. One time Clark Terry himself was the victim of this prank. Returning to the stage after a break, Terry picked up his horn for a big solo. But when he blew into it, nothing came out. He knew immediately what was wrong. But who had done it? Everyone in the band blamed Darby Hicks.

Terry, however, had his own suspicions. He threatened to kill one of his saxophonists, but he picked the wrong one. Six years later Marsalis finally admitted his guilt. "Clark," he disclosed in *Down Beat* magazine, "it was me who switched your valves during intermission! (. . . I didn't have the heart to confess.)"[10]

But there were more serious pastimes as well. Marsalis spent many sleepless late-night bus or plane trips discussing the jazz artists whose work he was studying so diligently—especially saxophonists John Coltrane and, "my guru at the time," Wayne Shorter.

In April 1981, while the Terry band was passing through New York City, Marsalis joined his father Ellis and brother Wynton in the studio to record one half of the Columbia album *Fathers and Sons*. (The remaining portion featured father-son saxophonists Von and Chico Freeman.)

Although he had gone back to the alto saxophone with Terry, Marsalis decided to leave the instrument in its case for this recording. Instead he used the slightly larger and more resonant sounding tenor saxophone that he played with Lionel Hampton's band. By the end of the year the tenor sax would become Marsalis' main horn.

When the Clark Terry gig ended in April, Marsalis spent a couple of tough months hanging around New York City and not finding much work. Surviving—barely—on just ten dollars a day, he was about to give up and return to New Orleans when he got calls from both drummer Elvin Jones and his first boss, Art Blakey. No longer leading a big band, Blakey had returned to his usual small-group format known as, the Jazz Messengers.

In the early 1960s Jones played behind John Coltrane, one of Marsalis' musical idols. The thought of working with "Trane's" drummer was a tempting one. Still he decided to take the gig with Blakey and return to the alto saxophone. Wynton, who had been on the road

31

with pianist Herbie Hancock, was about to rejoin the Jazz Messengers, and Branford wanted to play with his brother again.

Although Marsalis had left Berklee in January, he now was enrolled in the toughest music school of them all—"the Art Blakey Conservatory of Jazz." From the early 1950s, when he formed his first Jazz Messengers combo, to his death in 1990, Blakey dedicated himself to hiring and training the best young jazz musicians he could find. The list of promising, but raw, talents who became seasoned players in his bands reads like a "who's who" of the last forty years in jazz.

Blakey's ex-sidemen often speak of him as a demanding and encouraging teacher. His "classrooms" were nightclubs and concert halls. And his "lessons" were taught before live audiences around the world. Blakey set high standards for his young players and insisted that they stretch the boundaries of their abilities.

Blakey also set and maintained high standards for himself. He was a master drummer, one of the most important innovators and influences on his instrument. He drove the ensemble and propelled the soloists as few other drummers could. And whatever the age difference might have been between himself and his band members, Blakey not only kept in step with, but always ran just a little ahead of, his young players.

According to Marsalis, Blakey helped him to master the complex character of jazz rhythm, and in particular,

In 1980, and again in 1981, Marsalis toured with drummer, bandleader, and master teacher Art Blakey.

that subtle quality known as "swing." As the title of an early 1930s Duke Ellington song—"It Don't Mean a Thing If It Ain't Got that Swing"—points out, the ability to swing is the litmus test that separates real jazz players from second-rate amateurs. "Rhythm is it," Marsalis declared. ". . . I understood how time worked when I left Art."[11]

That summer Marsalis made another album with Blakey, *Keystone 3,* on the Concord Jazz label. This live recording offers a taste of the still-maturing saxophonist's early style and earned Blakey a Grammy nomination. In time the Marsalis brothers would be nominated for plenty of Grammy Awards in their own right.

Blakey, it is said, not only trained musicians, he produced *leaders* as well. When a player was ready to leave the Jazz Messengers, he also was ready to front his own group. By mid-summer of 1981 Wynton Marsalis decided it was time to graduate from the Blakey "academy." He was about to form a band, and he asked his older brother to join him. Naturally Branford agreed.

In just one year Branford Marsalis had worked with three jazz masters—Art Blakey, Lionel Hampton, and Clark Terry. Now, by becoming a key member of his brother's new group, he was about to take the next big step in his budding career. He knew that he still had a lot to learn. Nevertheless Marsalis was doing pretty well for someone who, just a short time earlier, didn't want to be a musician.

"He's the Leader"

By August 1981 Wynton Marsalis had left Art Blakey and rejoined Herbie Hancock's quartet for a tour of Japan. This brief gig, however, was really just a stopover for the nineteen-year-old trumpeter. He was preparing to launch a solo career, leading his own combo.

During this Japanese tour, Wynton was scheduled to do a recording session and he wanted Branford there with him. And so after four months with Blakey, the saxophonist resigned from the Jazz Messengers, flew to Japan, and joined his brother in Tokyo's CBS/Sony studio. Backed by an all-star rhythm section—Hancock on piano, Ron Carter on bass, and Tony Williams on drums—they recorded several selections for Wynton's debut album as a leader.

Because Wynton wanted the fuller, deeper sound of

the tenor saxophone in his group, he convinced Branford to put down the alto and take up the larger horn. As it turned out, Branford also preferred the tenor. "It's the closest instrument to the human voice in terms of depth and the ability to move a person," he once observed.[1] Since the end of 1981 the tenor sax has been Branford's primary instrument.

When the tour with Hancock was finished, Wynton asked his brother to help him put together his new quintet. Branford recruited his old Berklee friend and classmate Jeff "Tain" Watts on drums, and the young, but already accomplished, pianist, Kenny Kirkland. Branford, Watts, and Kirkland formed the nucleus of Wynton's group for most of the next four years. The band employed a succession of bassists before finally settling on Detroit's Robert Hurst a couple of years later.

Back in CBS's New York City studio, the new group recorded the remainder of Wynton's first album. Titled simply *Wynton Marsalis* and released on the Columbia label, it was one of the most successful jazz recordings of 1982.

The new Wynton Marsalis quintet created a sensation. It helped usher in what some critics have called "the jazz revival," and just in time. The music, for several reasons, was mired in a serious, decade-long slump.

At the end of the 1950s musicians such as saxophonists Ornette Coleman and John Coltrane, and pianist Cecil Taylor, among others, founded the avant-garde, or "free jazz," movement. They produced highly creative and demanding music, but their audience was small. Casual listeners found this music confusing. And many older jazz fans, who were raised on earlier styles, just didn't like it.

Then in the late 1960s, trumpeter Miles Davis turned jazz toward a new electronic-oriented, rock-inspired direction. This developed into what became known as "fusion" music. Ten years later, however, Davis had temporarily left the scene. And the music of even his most talented fusion followers began to sound stale and repetitious.

As the 1970s came to a close, creative jazz was facing a crisis of survival. Nightclubs had been closing since the early 1960s. The smaller, jazz-oriented record companies were folding, and the larger ones were severely cutting back their jazz divisions. It was the decade of disco—disposable, "fast food" music with plenty of flash, but little substance.

Many of America's top jazz artists had moved to Europe, where employment opportunities were more plentiful. Some took teaching positions in colleges and universities located in towns such as Oberlin, Ohio, or Bennington, Vermont. These small communities may have been pleasant places to live, but they were far removed from the big urban centers where, historically, jazz has gotten its inspiration.

Still other jazz musicians found work in the Hollywood or New York City recording studios, writing or playing on movie soundtracks, commercial jingles, or backgrounds for pop records. The music was rarely satisfying, but the money was good and the work was steady.

Then along came the Wynton Marsalis quintet. On the bandstand, dressed in their sharp suits, these talented youngsters displayed an air of professionalism and an impressive level of technical ability—what jazz musicians call "chops." Their slightly updated version of 1950s jazz, known as "hard bop," excited hard-core jazz fans, who longed for the return of non-electronic music. At the same time the quintet also caught the ears of many new listeners, who were looking for something more substantial than rock, fusion, or disco.

Wynton, labelled "the serious one" by the *New York Times*'s Peter Watrous,[2] appealed to an intellectually-inclined audience, the kind of people who like to study and analyze music, books, or films. Branford, "the loose one," attracted people who just want to have a good time when they go out. In Wynton's hands, jazz was profound; in Branford's hands, jazz was fun. Their opposite personalities actually complemented each other.

Of course it would be an exaggeration to claim that Wynton and Branford Marsalis "saved" jazz from extinction in the early 1980s. There was plenty of creative music being made by jazz artists, and their audiences—although small—were loyal.

Nevertheless the jazz revival was real. The big record labels once again started paying attention to the music. Newcomers who, like the Marsalis brothers, were still in their early twenties, were signed to recording contracts. Soon the critics began talking about a "young lions" movement in jazz.

At the same time many veteran players returned to the scene, performing live and making records—in many cases, for the first time in years. New jazz nightclubs opened in cities all over the country, and radio stations featuring a jazz format sprang up on the FM dial.

Jazz will never again be America's popular music, as it was in the big band era of the 1930s and 1940s. But at least it is being enjoyed by a wider audience once more, thanks, in large part, to the influence of the Marsalis brothers.

Obviously Branford was a key contributor to the Wynton Marsalis quintet and the impact that it had on the jazz world. However he insists that their success was the result of Wynton's vision alone. "I didn't see it coming," Branford admits. "I owe it all to my brother. He made it happen."[3]

The band's pianist, Kenny Kirkland, agrees. Wynton, although over a year younger, had more professional experience, and was more certain of what he wanted to do. "Branford didn't seem like the older brother," Kirkland observes. "He was under Wynton's tutelage. . . . It was Wynton's band."[4]

And so one has to wonder what it was like for Branford, working in his younger brother's band, looking on while Wynton got the lion's share of the attention. It was, he claims, a relief. "I sit down and watch him doing all of this," he told *Down Beat* in 1982, "and say, 'Yeah, great . . . somebody's gotta be in the hot seat. Better him than me.' "[5]

Even when they were kids back in New Orleans, Wynton always thrived under pressure. Branford, on the other hand, did best when people left him alone. So he decided to sit back and observe while his younger brother dealt with record companies, agents, managers, publicists, club owners, critics, and all the other non-musical facets of the music business. This way, he reasoned, when it was time for him to have his own band—and even then, he knew that day would come—he would have learned from Wynton's experiences.

Still it was true that these two brothers, with their different personalities, did not always see eye-to-eye, especially on musical matters. If it had been up to Branford, the quintet would have included more fusion and funk elements in its music. Wynton, however, preferred to stay in a strictly straight-ahead jazz groove.

"A lot of music he doesn't like," Branford explained at the time, "I like. . . . He's kind of set in his ways." So how did they resolve their musical disagreements? "It's simple," Branford responded, "he's the leader."[6]

The Wynton Marsalis quintet spent 1982 and the early part of 1983 performing in packed nightclubs and concert halls, and winning awards. They were the hottest new group—perhaps group, period—in jazz.

During the summer of 1983, the brothers took a brief break from the band to join pianist Herbie Hancock's VSOP (Very Special One-Time Performance) II quintet on a worldwide tour. The group included Ron Carter on bass and Tony Williams on drums, whom Wynton had performed with two summers ago. For Branford, however, touring with this kind of all-star band was a new and terrifying experience. He felt intimidated in their presence, and his playing showed it.

"You could not imagine the fear," he recalled in a *Rolling Stone* interview almost five years later. "It was so bad that two weeks into the tour Ron [Carter] said to me, 'We're delighted by the fact that you're in awe of us. But we're paying you money to play, and you ain't playin'.'"[7] The saxophonist managed to pull himself together for the remainder of the tour, but, barely twenty-three years old, he realized that he still had a lot to learn about playing jazz.

During that summer Wynton's second album, *Think of One,* featuring his brother on tenor and soprano saxophones, was released. Once the VSOP II tour was over the trumpeter reassembled his quintet, and

Branford resumed his role as Wynton's supporting player.

But Branford was beginning to step out from his younger brother's long shadow. He already had begun working on his own debut album as a leader. The recording, titled *Scenes in the City* and featuring three of Marsalis' original compositions, was released by Columbia in April 1984.

The material on *Scenes in the City* could be called "modern mainstream," straight-ahead jazz that was in no way far-out or radical. It presented Marsalis in a variety of settings, from trio to septet, and with varying personnel that included many of jazz's finest young players—trombonist Robin Eubanks, pianists Kenny Kirkland and Mulgrew Miller, bassist Charnett Moffett, and drummers Jeff "Tain" Watts and Marvin "Smitty" Smith. Bassist Ron Carter, whose constructive criticism had helped to motivate Marsalis on the VSOP II tour, also performed on some of the tracks.

Reviewer Michael Ullman, in *High Fidelity*, wished that Marsalis had taken more musical risks on his debut album. Although, he noted, *Scenes in the City* was not as conservative as Wynton's first two recordings, Ullman felt that it still was "probably not wild enough for those who see him as the 'soulful' Marsalis."[8]

Down Beat's J. B. Figi was more enthusiastic. In his opinion the new recording showed that Marsalis is "one of the most promising saxophonists about, displaying chops, intelligence, and a loose, unforced style." As for whether or not he had played it too safe, the reviewer stated bluntly, "The material may be routine; the playing isn't." But Figi added that there was room for improvement, for growth. "As good as he is, Marsalis seems less than fully formed."[9]

Most observers took that same wait-and-see attitude toward Marsalis. "Who is he?" asked Eric Levin, reviewing the album in *People.* It was a reasonable question. You couldn't expect a twenty-four-year-old musician to have developed a mature musical identity of his own. That comes only with experience.

So the critics gave Marsalis credit for making a strong start, and wondered where it would lead him. "He's earned our interest in the next phase of his education," Levin concluded, "when whatever discoveries there will be must come from within."[10]

With his first recording on the market, Marsalis began making occasional appearances in front of his own quartet, consisting of Smith on drums, Moffett on bass, and pianist Larry Willis. Critic Stuart Troup saw the group at New York City's Village Vanguard—and expressed what many listeners had begun to feel. "A player like Branford Marsalis," he wrote, "leading a dynamite group like this one, . . . says everything we want to hear about the future of jazz."[11]

Marsalis also made a brief guest appearance on Miles Davis's album *Decoy,* playing soprano saxophone. Davis

For almost four years Branford Marsalis worked in his brother Wynton's quintet. Here Branford and Wynton are joined by their proud father, Ellis Marsalis.

actually wanted Marsalis to join his band, "but he couldn't do it," the trumpeter said in his 1989 autobiography, "because he was committed to playing with his brother Wynton."[12]

Although he was getting recording projects and gigs on his own, Branford still was a member of the Wynton Marsalis quintet, at least for the time being. The group had its own 1984 release, *Hot House Flowers,* toured Japan in November, and the following January, went back into the studio to record *Black Codes (From the Underground).* But that would be Branford's final album with Wynton.

The year 1985 marked both a breakthrough in Marsalis' career and a break—professionally and personally—with Wynton. Branford sensed that, after nearly four years, he had gone as far as he could under his younger brother's leadership. He had ideas of his own that he wanted to pursue. Ironically it was Wynton's example that gave Branford the confidence he needed to make the move.

"He helped me take responsibility for things," Marsalis notes, "helped me realize that my life is mine to live or not. . . . I figured that my potential is mine to be fulfilled. So why not fulfill it?"[13] By spring Branford would leave Wynton's group and begin to follow his own creative path. It would be, for a jazz musician, an unusual and controversial route.

"I Play What I Like"

"The pressure's been getting to me," Branford Marsalis told *Down Beat* in mid-1985 only half-kiddingly. ". . . I've been flying, playing, flying, playing, different town every night."[1] That was just a slight exaggeration.

For example, on April 26, Wynton's quintet—with Branford on saxophone—opened the New Orleans Jazz and Heritage Festival, appearing on the same bill with Miles Davis. Although neither brother knew it at the time, this would be their farewell performance together. Marsalis then flew to New Jersey for a week-long gig with his own group. Next he played a one-nighter in the "Salsa Meets Jazz" series at New York City's Village Gate.

Normally "the sports junkie of doom,"[2] as he calls himself, would have stayed in the city for a few days and caught a couple of Mets games. Instead Marsalis jetted off to Paris, where he married Teresa Reese, an actress-singer whom he had met in 1980 when they were students at Berklee. While in France he appeared in a musical film. During a three-day break in the shooting, he skipped over to London, England, to record a classical album. And then he hit the road with Sting.

Sting? The ex-guitarist and lead singer with the rock band The Police? Branford Marsalis, young lion of jazz, was touring with a rock star? Much of the jazz world was shocked at the news. Marsalis, however, never thought of himself as a jazz purist.

"I hate pop music," he once joked with an interviewer, "as you can see by looking at these worn, faded rock and roll records."[3] He still kept—and enjoyed—albums he first listened to as a teenager, records by such "unjazz-like" performers as Steely Dan, Led Zeppelin, James Brown, and Pink Floyd.

When Marsalis met Sting in early 1985, the singer said that he wanted to put together a new band to record and tour with. Marsalis told him that the best musicians he knew were jazz musicians. And so Sting asked him to assemble—and, of course, play saxophone in—the new band, just as Wynton had done three and a half years earlier.

Marsalis brought in bassist Daryl Jones, who was with Miles Davis; drummer Omar Hakim, from the fusion group Weather Report; and a colleague out of the

Wynton Marsalis quintet, Kenny Kirkland on keyboards. It was, in Marsalis' opinion, "the ultimate pop band. There was literally never a bad night."[4] They proved it in February when Sting and his new group played three sold-out shows at the Ritz in New York City.

In March, Sting took the musicians into a studio in Barbados to record *The Dream of the Blue Turtles,* an eventual multimillion seller. When it was released later that year many reviewers agreed with Jim Miller of *Newsweek,* who felt that Marsalis was "the real standout" on the album.[5]

May found the band in France, where they appeared in a feature-length documentary titled *Bring on the Night.* Although the film naturally focused on Sting, many people—including Sting himself—thought that Marsalis and his wisecracking comments stole the show. "There was only one leading man in that film—and it wasn't me," the singer concedes.[6]

Marsalis and Kirkland returned to the United States after making the film, expecting to rejoin Wynton's group. Instead they found that they had been replaced—in effect, fired. Unlike his brother, Wynton did not have a very high opinion of pop music or musicians. "I didn't spend all those years practicing my horn," the trumpeter told *Jet* magazine bluntly, "trying to develop as a musician . . . just to pantomime behind somebody who sings out of tune."[7]

In 1985 Marsalis shocked much of the jazz world, and even his own family, when he began performing with rock singer-musician Sting.

Branford previously had tried to reassure his brother. "I've been getting some grief from Wynton," he admitted at the time, "but I told him this is the one and only time I'm gonna play rock and roll."[8] But Wynton, a jazz purist if there ever was one, could not understand how real jazz musicians could work with a rock star. It was like "Bo Jackson playing Little League," he said.[9]

The rest of the Marsalis clan agreed. "My whole family gave Branford a rough time about it," his brother Delfeayo revealed.[10] For a while Branford downplayed the firing, claiming, "It was just business. It wasn't a feud."[11] But later he acknowledged that "it was acrimonious at times. . . . It was a painful thing."[12]

Since then the Marsalis brothers have patched up their differences. "Me and Wynton, that's a dead issue," Branford insists. "He knows who I am and accepts that."[13] For his part, Wynton seems to have softened his view of pop music. "I used to think that was all a waste of time," he says, "but now I realize that different types of music have different functions."[14]

On July 13, 1985, Marsalis appeared with Sting at the "Live Aid" concert, an all-day, all-star rock extravaganza organized to raise money to fight hunger in Africa. Performing before 90,000 people in London's Wembley Stadium and a worldwide television audience estimated in the hundreds of millions, Sting delivered a relaxed, intimate set of tunes—backed by Marsalis' saxophone—that was one of the highlights of this historic event. In

August the band was off to Japan to open an eight-month world tour that ended in Paris the following March.

Marsalis took on his most challenging non-musical role—the role of a father—in November, when his son, Reese, was born. As a working musician on the road for weeks—even months—at a time, Marsalis had to spend much of his son's early years away from him. And so he learned to treasure the time that he could be with Reese, and he often took the boy with him to recording sessions and video shoots.

He quickly realized that raising a child is a huge responsibility. "If you do a bad job as a parent," Marsalis explains with a mixture of awe and anxiety, "you've ruined another human being. It's the scariest thing that I can ever think of. But I wouldn't trade it for anything else in the world."[15]

Much of the jazz world, including most of his own family, felt that the new father had traded jazz for rock. They shook their heads and murmured that Marsalis was "wasting his talent." But in at least one way, he maintains, working with Sting "made me a better musician. . . . I was more confident in my ability."[16] Kenny Kirkland agrees. "He found his own voice with Sting—it made him more aggressive and confident."[17]

At the same time Marsalis feels that, compared with jazz, rock is a much less demanding type of music. "With Sting," he observed, "I have to streamline everything I play."[18] In other words, when you are backing a singer, you have to stay out of the way and simplify your playing. There is no room for the kind of complex, extended solos that are common in jazz.

And so his playing gained a much needed aggressiveness on the Sting tour; when it was over, however, Marsalis had to resharpen his jazz "chops." He never cared much for practicing but now he realized it was necessary. "I was able to get more technique when I got off the tour and came back to playing jazz and practicing constantly," he explains.[19]

Marsalis also observed some extra-musical differences between jazz and rock. "You know what a rock-and-roll tour is?" he asked an interviewer. "It's airport, van, hotel, van, venue, van, airport." This is not, he argues, a very stimulating environment in which to be a musician.

"In jazz," he contrasts, "it's hotel, sound check, mall—hang out, video game—concert, end of concert, meet the people, jam session or nightclub or hangout scene or restaurant."[20] Because jazz tours are less structured than rock-and-roll tours, you can spend time with other musicians and fans. Marsalis clearly prefers the jazz environment.

As a jazz musician Marsalis often finds it frustrating being around many of the rock performers whom he meets. "These guys are just selling records," he comments. "They're not musicians, just businessmen.

They're affable folk, but you can't talk music with them, you talk business. I like *music*."[21]

Marsalis enjoyed his first tour with Sting—and respected Sting's musicianship—but after it ended, he jumped back into jazz. Through the summer of 1986, he traveled the United States, Europe, and Japan with a stellar rhythm section: pianist Herbie Hancock, bassist Ron Carter, and Al Foster (later Tony Williams) on drums. The last time Marsalis worked with these veteran players—the 1983 VSOP II tour—he was intimidated by them. Now, thanks to his newfound confidence, "I felt like a peer, not a subordinate."[22]

Marsalis also recorded his second jazz album, *Royal Garden Blues*. "I wanted to do a jazz record in the middle of a pop tour," he explains, "because I heard so many disparaging remarks—'You guys think you can play jazz at the same time you play pop. . . . It doesn't work.' I thought, 'OK, we'll see how right they are.' "

Royal Garden Blues proved the doubters were wrong. Still, Marsalis feels that it would have been better to wait a few months before going into the studio. "My chops had fallen off, definitely. I was really struggling to get my control together; the direction I take on the solos is real strange."[23] Nevertheless the album, which features guest pianist Ellis Marsalis on one tune, was a top-seller and earned Branford a Grammy nomination in the "Best Jazz Instrumental Performance, Soloist" category.

Meanwhile the saxophonist kept up his double life.

His second album with Sting, a live recording titled *Bring on the Night,* was released. "Branford Marsalis is the real star of the proceedings," wrote *Jazziz's* reviewer, William D. White. ". . . His music conception has just the right mix of drive and sophistication to nudge Sting's space age rockers off the ground and really fly."[24]

There was also something very different—a new album of classical music titled *Romances for Saxophone.* Playing soprano saxophone, and backed by the English Chamber Orchestra, Marsalis performed pieces by such revered composers as Igor Stravinsky, Claude Debussy, Maurice Ravel, and Erik Satie. Strange as it might sound, the album was a "hit," spending over two months among the top five recordings on *Billboard* magazine's classical chart. Jazz, rock, and now classical—"Man, this is a *triple* life," he proclaimed.[25]

Although jazz would always be his first love, Marsalis continued his fling with popular music. He toured with Sting again in 1987 and 1988. This time he learned to take advantage of all the down time by practicing or composing. He has recorded twice more with Sting—on the 1987 release . . . *Nothing Like the Sun* and the 1991 *The Soul Cages.* Marsalis also has performed on albums by Tina Turner and the Grateful Dead, played a saxophone solo on Public Enemy's rap hit, "Fight the Power," and appeared with Gang Starr on the cable TV program, *Yo! MTV Raps.*

Many jazz diehards still raise their eyebrows and

shake their heads at Marsalis' pop connections. But he isn't betraying jazz, the saxophonist argues. He's just being true to his unusually broad musical tastes. "I play what I like," Marsalis insists. "I am a jazz musician, but sometimes I play rock. For some reason that makes people mad."[26] They'll just have to get used to it.

New Doors

In his career Branford Marsalis has chosen to do many different things, and he has done all of them well. "I practiced to be a funk musician," he told *Ebony* magazine in 1989, "then I joined a jazz band. I became a jazz musician, and once I had played jazz for five years, what do I do? I join a rock band and do movies."[1]

Yes, *movies*—all sorts of new doors seem to keep opening for Marsalis. Actor-director Danny DeVito saw his scene-stealing bits in *Bring on the Night* and gave the musician a small role in his 1987 comedy *Throw Momma From the Train*. "He's exactly the way he is on film—very loose, very genuine," DeVito observes. "He's a cool guy, Branford."[2]

Hot, young filmmaker Spike Lee gave Marsalis a small part in his early 1988 release, *School Daze*. "I said to Spike," he recalls, " 'If you're stupid enough to think I can do it, I'm stupid enough to screw up your movie for you.' "[3] But he needn't have worried. Using the improvising skills that, as a jazz musician, he acquired over the years, Marsalis devised a fistfight scene. Lee thought the bit was funny enough to leave in the film. "Branford's a leader," the director remarked.[4]

Lee also directed Marsalis' music video, "Royal Garden Blues," the title track from his second album. And in 1987 the saxophonist appeared in a short feature film, *Horn of Plenty,* that Lee made for NBC's *Saturday Night Live* show.

Marsalis and Lee have become good friends, bound by a common love—sports. While Marsalis was living in New York City he had a season box at Shea Stadium. It was not unusual to see Marsalis and Lee together at New York Mets games. "When I go to Shea with Spike Lee," the saxophonist laughs, "I pretend to be his bodyguard—'Give the man some space!' "[5]

But Marsalis probably didn't see as many games as he would have wanted to that season. As usual he spent much of the summer of 1987 on the road, touring Europe in July and Japan in August with pianist Kenny Kirkland, bassist Delbert Felix, and drummer Lewis Nash.

In September his third jazz album, *Renaissance,* was released. For the first time Marsalis made an entire recording, except for one unaccompanied solo track, with the same group of musicians—Kenny Kirkland, bassist Robert Hurst (on loan from Wynton's group), and Tony Williams on drums. For this reason *Renaissance* has a coherence that Marsalis' previous releases lack. It sounds like a well-planned musical statement rather than merely a collection of songs.

The new recording gave strong evidence that the saxophonist's playing was continuing to grow and evolve. On tenor, Marsalis used a dark, rich sound; on soprano, he drew from a broad palette of tone colors—bright, sad, light-hearted, or brooding. Perhaps he still was "searching for his own voice" and maybe there were a few "unfocused passages," as reviewer Geoffrey Himes wrote in *The Washington Post*. But *Renaissance* also contained, Himes pointed out, "moments of sudden, unforced eloquence."[6]

Typically, Marsalis was not completely satisfied. "I'm making records I enjoy," he remarked shortly after the album's release, "but they're not groundbreaking." He was right. Although *Renaissance* was a fine recording, it bore the marks of other saxophonists, notably Ben Webster, Sonny Rollins, John Coltrane, and Wayne Shorter—Marsalis' main musical influences at the time. It did not reveal enough about who Branford Marsalis was and what *he* had to say.

But he was not frustrated. Marsalis understood that jazz musicians often invest years of study, practice, and self-exploration before forging a truly original style. "I know I have ideas that are unique and haven't been done before," he maintained. "One day I'll deal with it."[7]

In the meantime there was more work with Sting. In October 1987 Marsalis and Sting appeared together on *Saturday Night Live.* The following January they launched a three-month American tour, and played three more months throughout Europe.

On June 11, 1988, Sting and Marsalis performed at the "Freedomfest" concert in support of Nelson Mandela, the then-imprisoned South African anti-apartheid leader. The concert was broadcast worldwide from Wembley Stadium in London. They began a new two-month tour of the United States and Canada in July. Later in the year Sting and the band did a tour for the human rights organization, Amnesty International, and taped an HBO special in Japan.

On the jazz side Marsalis made a guest appearance on the album *Digital Duke* with the Duke Ellington Orchestra, which is directed by the late pianist-composer's son, Mercer. His solo on the classic 1940s Ellington tune, "Cotton Tail," earned Marsalis a second Grammy nomination ("Best Jazz Instrumental Performance, Soloist") in 1988.

June brought the release of a new album, made in Japan the previous summer and titled *Random Abstract.* To Marsalis, who like many musicians is his own harshest critic, it was "a compromise record." Instead of using the players that he would have preferred, "I had to go with what was available," the musicians with whom he was on tour at the time.

"[Drummer] Lewis Nash and [bassist] Delbert Felix are definitely great musicians," he explained. ". . . But we didn't have the kind of intellectual relationship that can really make the music take off."[8] Because jazz is so heavily improvised, the interplay among the members of the group is crucial. By the time *Random Abstract* came out, Marsalis was working with what, he felt, was a more compatible rhythm section. Old friend Kenny Kirkland remained on piano, joined by bassist Robert Hurst and drummer Jeff "Tain" Watts.

Nevertheless *Stereo Review*'s Chris Albertson announced, "If anyone asks you what musicians mean when they say a group is 'cooking,' I suggest that you play them the opening track, 'Yes and No,' of Branford Marsalis' new album." Even on the slower tunes, Albertson added, "there isn't a dull or uninspired moment."[9] *Random Abstract* earned Grammy nominations in both the "Best Jazz Instrumental Performance, Soloist," and "Best Jazz Instrumental Performance, Group" categories.

At the end of 1988 composer Bill Lee (Spike Lee's father) called on Marsalis to perform some of the music that he had written for the sound track of his son's upcoming film, *Do the Right Thing.* Marsalis' solo saxophone rendering of "Lift Every Voice and Sing," known by long-time civil rights activists as "the black

Marsalis enjoys making different kinds of music with a wide variety
of musicians. Here he, bassist Robert Hurst and drummer Jeff
"Tain" Watts jam with blues great B.B. King.

national anthem," served as a musical prelude to Lee's popular and controversial movie about racism.

May 19, 1989, marked what Marsalis calls, "one of the most thrilling achievements of my career."[10] Tenor saxophone giant Sonny Rollins, then fifty-nine years old, had asked Marsalis, who at twenty-eight was less than half Rollins' age, to perform with him in concert at New York City's Carnegie Hall. "I have the greatest respect for Branford," Rollins said. "I wanted to choose someone compatible."

Marsalis was both honored and awed by the opportunity to play alongside the legendary "saxophone colossus." But he knew that he was facing a tough test. Rollins, especially in his live performances, is a formidable force. "It's like going in the ring with Mike Tyson," Marsalis mused. ". . . A lot of cats said, 'Man, I would never take that gig'—but he didn't ask them. . . . And I figure," he added philosophically, "what's wrong with getting slaughtered by Sonny Rollins?"[11]

According to the *New York Times*'s reviewer Jon Pareles that is exactly what happened. "Poor Mr. Marsalis," he reported. "When he joined the group, offering solos that would sound thoughtful and shapely elsewhere, Mr. Rollins outgunned him with a mixture of raw vitality and a higher calculus of harmony." But Pareles noted, it was not really Marsalis' fault, since "when Mr. Rollins is in such remarkable form, hardly a musician alive could keep up with him."[12]

For his part Marsalis is grateful for the experience. "The ultimate way to learn this music is to watch it being performed," he observes. "I learned this for sure when Sonny Rollins was chopping me up onstage. . . . All of the things that make Rollins's playing logical I understood in that hour and a half."[13] He may have gotten "slaughtered," but he would be a better musician for it.

Two weeks later Marsalis joined Rollins in the studio to record two selections on Rollins's album, *Falling in Love with Jazz*. Marsalis played well, as he did in the Carnegie Hall concert, but again he was overshadowed by the raw power and musical energy of the veteran saxophonist.

Marsalis' own new album, a two-record set titled *Trio Jeepy*, was released that June. His first recording without a piano, it featured Jeff "Tain" Watts on drums and one of jazz's most admired elder statesmen—the then seventy-eight-year-old bassist Milt Hinton. (Delbert Felix took Hinton's place on three tracks.)

Produced on the fly just before he went out on the road with Sting in early 1988, this was not the album Marsalis really wanted to make. He would have preferred to wait until the tour was over, and he had time to get his "jazz chops" back.

However that would have created a two-year lapse between releases. In the highly competitive music business, two years is a very long time. Marsalis didn't want jazz fans to start wondering, "What ever happened to Branford?" So he felt that he should get *something* out right away.

"I didn't have a band," Marsalis revealed in *Down Beat* nearly three years later, "so I called up Milt and we went into the studio [with Watts]. . . . Really we just went in and had a jam session." And that is how much of the album sounds—loosely organized, under-rehearsed, and inconsistent. To this always self-critical saxophonist, *Trio Jeepy* "wasn't my idea of a great record at all."[14]

Down Beat's reviewer, Art Lange, gave the album just two and a half stars (out of a possible five). He felt that the group's playing was "aimless" and criticized Marsalis' performance in particular. "There is no sense that he *feels* these songs very deeply," Lange wrote. On the whole the critic concluded, "Releasing these flat, flawed performances was a mistake, and does a disservice to the talents of the musicians, especially Branford."[15]

But Geoffrey Himes of *The Washington Post* saw *Trio Jeepy* in a somewhat more positive light. He noted that the album "definitely has its moments" and praised Marsalis as "a wonderful melodic improviser who always keeps in mind the singability of the solos."[16] Whatever its flaws *Trio Jeepy* sold well, climbing to number five on *Billboard's* jazz charts, and was nominated for a Grammy in the "Best Jazz Instrumental Performance, Group" category.

The summer of 1989 found Marsalis again on tour, following the festival circuit through the United States, Canada, and Brazil. He was pleased to be working again with his preferred rhythm team of Kirkland, Hurst, and Watts.

And this time he had a surprise for the critics and audiences. His music had taken a new turn—freer, more complex, and decidedly original. Branford Marsalis was finding his own musical voice.

Crazy People Music

"Those of you who want to hear tunes from my last album should go home and play it," Branford Marsalis sometimes told audiences during the summer of 1989. He wasn't trying to be rude or arrogant. He was just letting the crowd know that his music was changing right before their ears, as it were. And so he might not be playing what they expected to hear.

Out of his various influences Marsalis finally had forged a way of playing that bore his personal imprint. Gone were the obvious traces of Sonny Rollins, John Coltrane, and Wayne Shorter. Or more accurately, these had been melded into a style that was identifiably and uniquely "Branford."

In jazz, he realized, true individuality comes only with time. "The real way to learn to play jazz," he has explained, "is to borrow a little bit from this guy, a little bit from that guy, and eventually it starts to sound like you."[1] Marsalis listened to the saxophone masters who came before him, studied their work, and absorbed what he needed. Now he was ready to join them as a major jazz voice in his own right.

Marsalis' mature style is hard-driving, compelling, and relentless. His playing has become more daring, freer, and less constricted. Marsalis likes to call it "crazy people music," because, he believes, that is what non-jazz fans think of it. And perhaps all those rapid bursts of notes do seem sort of disconnected at first hearing. Upon closer examination, however, you can see that Marsalis' solos are coherent and completely logical.

The Branford Marsalis quartet opened 1990 with six straight sold-out concerts in Japan. In February he was back in the United States to perform the national anthem at the NBA all-star game. The next day he, along with Sting, Herbie Hancock, Bruce Springsteen, Paul Simon, and many other music stars, appeared at a benefit concert in Los Angeles for the Rain Forest Foundation—Sting's favorite environmental cause.

Marsalis ventured back into rock and roll that March when he joined the Grateful Dead for a concert at the Nassau Coliseum in Long Island, New York. At year's end he was on the opposite coast, jamming with the Dead at its annual New Year's Eve bash in the Oakland-Alameda Coliseum.

He enjoys the Dead's free-wheeling, improvised type of rock and roll. And the Dead respect the way Marsalis challenges them musically. "Such a musician—we're almost good enough to keep up with him," declared chief Dead-head Jerry Garcia before a 1991 concert.[2]

When Spike Lee was casting his film, *Mo' Better Blues,* a story about jazz musicians, he offered Marsalis the important supporting role of saxophone player "Shadow Henderson." Marsalis, however, turned Lee down because "I didn't think I was good enough to do justice to the part; it was pretty meaty stuff."[3] Instead he dubbed the saxophone parts for actor Wesley Snipes, and composed three original pieces for the film's soundtrack—which also featured the rest of his quartet, plus Terence Blanchard on trumpet.

When *Mo' Better Blues* hit the theaters that summer it received only lukewarm reviews. Nevertheless most critics complimented the music—written by Marsalis, Blanchard, and Bill Lee. Some felt it was one of the few strong elements in an otherwise disappointing movie.

As a professional jazz musician Marsalis thought that parts of Lee's film lacked realism, especially the nightclub scenes. "Ain't no clubs look that good!" he complained. ". . . Gimme a break, man. Give *me* a break. No one ever yawns and the whole audience is black? . . . I told him not to do that."[4]

Branford Marsalis at work on the soundtrack music for Spike Lee's 1989 film, *Mo' Better Blues*—front row: Branford Marsalis and Kenny Kirkland; back row: Bill Lee, Spike Lee, Jeff "Tain" Watts, and Terence Blanchard.

A few days before the movie opened in early August, the soundtrack album, *Music from Mo' Better Blues,* was released under Marsalis' name. His new quartet recording, *Crazy People Music,* came out simultaneously.

At last Marsalis was able to make an album with his "band from heaven"—Kenny Kirkland, Robert Hurst, and Jeff "Tain" Watts—and the results were extremely impressive. Working together as a solid, cohesive unit, the quartet creates a tightly-knit group music. Marsalis' own playing is free, complex, and highly personal. This was not just his best work to date. It was his breakthrough recording, and he knew it.

"Now we're a band," Marsalis explained, "and working things out the way bands can. The only record . . . that approaches it was *Random Abstract,* and that's because that was also a working band." But that really was not the band he had wanted to use. Although most people felt that *Random Abstract* was a good album, in Marsalis' opinion it was not good enough.

Thanks to Kirkland, Hurst, and Watts, *Crazy People Music* finally achieved the high level of musical unity that Marsalis was seeking. In short, the album was better because the band was better. Still the saxophonist managed to find something to criticize. "The record is not as good as the band is live," he claimed, "but isn't that the way it always turns out?"[5]

Chris Albertson evaluated both new Marsalis releases for *Stereo Review.* He noted that the soundtrack album contained some good jazz, but was "diluted" by the presence of pop and rap. "In between these atrocities," he commented caustically, "lie some fine performances by Blanchard and the Marsalis group, but they only account for 17½ minutes of this skimpy 38-minute offering."

Albertson was far more enthusiastic about *Crazy People Music.* "A solid 65 minutes of excellent hard bop—and sounds beyond that—played by a group that enjoys unusual rapport. If Branford Marsalis continues along this path," the critic declared, "he will firmly establish himself in the upper echelon of jazz artists." In short, he concluded, "*Crazy People Music* is much mo' better than the soundtrack."[6]

Marsalis agreed with that assessment. "The music for *Mo' Better* is obviously not all jazz," he insisted, "even though people say it is." He knew that a large portion of the movie's audience probably would not be dedicated jazz fans. And so, Marsalis explained, "We simplified it so that the average person could understand it. . . . The quartet record is hard-core jazz with not a lot of recognizable melodies."[7] It was clear which one he preferred.

Nevertheless the more "middle of the road" soundtrack album outsold the bolder *Crazy People Music* nearly four to one—a fact that seemed to disappoint Marsalis. "I don't expect anything anymore," he said with resignation. "I play the music I choose to play, and

I'm happy doing that. If people don't like it, that's cool."[8]

It's not that Marsalis was turning his back on the wider audience. He simply decided to abide by his integrity as an artist. And since he has been able to make a good living playing jazz, there is no point in "selling out."

"I don't need a million dollars to be happy," Marsalis maintains. "I just want to play music and be with my family and have enough to pay for my house and car."[9] So he keeps on playing his "crazy people music" and hoping that other crazy people will enjoy it.

In any event, the following winter both recordings were honored with Grammy nominations. *Crazy People Music* was named in the "Best Jazz Instrumental Performance, Soloist" category. A track off *Music from Mo' Better Blues,* "Again Never" by Marsalis' quartet with Terence Blanchard, was nominated for the "Best Jazz Instrumental Performance, Group" Grammy.

Marsalis made another film soundtrack appearance in 1990. In Australian director Fred Schoepsi's movie, *The Russia House,* Sean Connery portrays a British spy who enjoys playing the soprano saxophone for relaxation. Schoepsi hired Marsalis to dub in the saxophone parts for Connery's character. He also was featured on the soundtrack to the 1992 comedy-thriller, *Sneakers.*

In all, Marsalis and his "crazy people" band spent

approximately three hundred days on the road in 1990, including a visit to the Moscow Jazz festival in June, a ten-country tour of Europe, and a return trip to Japan late in the year. But in October he took a brief break from his schedule to join the rest of the Marsalis family in a benefit concert for the Autism Society. It was a cause that was close to all of their hearts—one of Branford's younger brothers, Mboya, is autistic.

Personally, Branford and Wynton Marsalis were again as close as ever, having resolved their professional differences. Musically, however, they were never further apart. During the previous year Wynton proclaimed that he had decided to re-examine traditional New Orleans jazz. And so the trumpeter's recent recording and live performances found him exploring and re-creating the oldest jazz forms and styles.

Branford, on the other hand, was looking ahead rather than backward. He knew and respected the music's foundations, as do all serious jazz artists. But instead of reconstructing them, as Wynton was doing, Branford, always the more adventurous brother, was building upon them.

As Peter Watrous, the *New York Times*'s jazz critic, has written, Marsalis and many of his contemporaries were attempting "to bring the past into the present, to take what one loves from the past and make it live again." This, he maintained, is "the first step toward something genuinely new."[10]

"A Charmed Life"

In 1991, for the second straight year, Branford Marsalis spent nearly three hundred days on the road. The life of a traveling musician may look exciting and glamorous. And it certainly is a thrill to be working on stage before hundreds, maybe thousands, of enthusiastic fans. But all most people see is the performance. What about the rest of it? What is *that* part of it like?

Life on the road is tough, to say the least. There is little time for the simple pleasures. You eat, but you rarely enjoy your meal. You sleep, but you seldom rest. And the travel never seems to end. There is always another gig in a day or two, one more place where you are expected to play—and play your best.

For instance, during one twenty-day stretch in 1992, shortly before he debuted as the new musical director of

The Tonight Show—and finally was able to come off the road—Marsalis and his group had the following itinerary:

March 27—Detroit, Michigan

28—College Station, Texas

29—Tulsa, Oklahoma

April 2—Potsdam, New York

3—Lewisburg, Pennsylvania

4—Buffalo, New York

7—Mexico City, Mexico

8-12—New York City, New York

14—Princetown, New Jersey

15—Durham, North Carolina

Ten different cities in twenty days—but that was hardly unusual. Starting on April 24 in Stamford, Connecticut, Marsalis hit the road again. He played seven cities in nine days, stopping in upstate New York, Wisconsin, Indiana, and Ohio before finishing on May 2 in Des Moines, Iowa.

Not only is life on the road exhausting, it also can be incredibly dull. You ride in vans when the gigs are nearby, or fly on planes for hours at a time. And so while traveling, Marsalis and his group would rely on a whole range of pastimes to help relieve the boredom.

They listened to cassettes, swapped "inside" stories about the music business and fellow musicians, and devoured a wide menu of snack foods—from donuts to blue-corn chips. And they spent an unknown number of hours trying to break the band record in "Tetris" on their Nintendo® Game Boys.

Marsalis, one of the world's biggest sports fans, loved to talk nonstop about whichever one of his favorite New York area teams—the Mets, Jets, or Knicks—happened to be in season at the moment. It didn't matter if anyone else in the band was interested. He would keep right on talking sports.

Musicians—even top professionals—must practice to stay sharp and keep their technique, their "chops," in shape. "I still have to work on it," Marsalis admits. "I need to practice, like an hour a day consistently."

Unfortunately the road allowed him little energy or opportunity for this. Being on tour is tiring and time-consuming, and performers are grateful for any break in the routine. "If I had three days off, I'd go to a game or to the movies," Marsalis explains. ". . . I'd eventually practice, but it wouldn't be at the top of my list."[1]

So why did he do it? "Going on the road is not fun," Marsalis emphasized at the time, "and if I didn't have to, I wouldn't be out here that much. But I really don't have an alternative." Like most jazz musicians he was faced with a difficult choice. He could work less, and enjoy more time with his family. However, if he did that, Marsalis realized, "I couldn't afford my home."[2]

And so as long as there were bills to pay, he kept

traveling—spending an average of only five days each month at home. Of course Marsalis was fortunate to be so busy, so sought-after. Most jazz musicians had far less work, and he knew it.

But Marsalis' motives were not only material ones. Although individual practice is hard to manage during a tour, the nightly gigs help sharpen a band's ability to perform collectively.

Marsalis had been touring regularly with the same musicians—Kenny Kirkland, Robert Hurst, and Jeff "Tain" Watts—since the summer of 1989. Spending all that time together helped to weld them into a solid, cohesive group. "We may not be the best musicians," the saxophonist remarked in late 1990, "but we're the best band. . . . We all understand each other, complement each other very well."[3]

Jazz is, after all, a group music. Each member of the band has to be attuned to what the other players are doing at all times. Musicians develop that sort of "sixth sense" only by working together constantly, and going on the road makes that possible.

And so Marsalis resigned himself to the life of a road warrior. "I think music is based on a continuing process," he maintained, "and if you stop, you stagnate. So I'm always gonna be on the road."[4] At least that's what he believed at the time.

Perhaps for Marsalis, the best part of traveling was being able to spend so much time with Kirkland, Hurst, and Watts. Not only does he respect them as musicians, he likes their company as friends. Over the years the Branford Marsalis quartet enjoyed its share of laughs, both on stage and off.

They even developed their own personal language, a strange combination of obscure phrases and knowing looks that only the four of them could understand. As Peter Watrous has written, to an uninitiated observer, "being with them is like being thrown in the middle of a secret society."[5]

Marsalis is, by nature, an easygoing character, a "regular guy." "He's a fun-loving person," says George Butler, the Columbia Records executive who signed both Branford and Wynton to that label, "who would be as content with McDonald's as any ritzy restaurant."[6]

His manner is normally friendly and relaxed, and his way of dressing is typically informal—T-shirts or sweatshirts, jeans or bermuda shorts, sneakers, and baseball cap. "I only get dressed up when I'm working," he told *Vogue* magazine.[7]

But when they are working Marsalis and his band usually are the height of fashion. In their tailored suits and the most stylish ties—the uniform of jazz's "young lions" ever since the first Wynton Marsalis quintet hit the scene in 1981—they look like they stepped right off the pages of *GQ*. "Wynton went through about twelve bass players with that first band," the saxophonist jokes. "Bad ties."[8]

Marsalis' informal nature and subtle sense of humor come through in his performances. He knows how to charm an audience, drawing them in and making them care about his music, however intense or unfamiliar it may seem. Marsalis can break up the crowd with a sly grin or a carefully timed glance as he once did during a gig at New York City's Village Vanguard. "After one of the sound system's many spasms," Watrous reported in *The New York Times,* "it took just a raised eyebrow to get the audience laughing."[9]

He also has a talent for ad-libbing clever little inside jokes when the situation calls for them. One time the band muffed its arrangement of the well-known standard "April in Paris." When the tune was over Marsalis announced the title as "April Embarrassed."

Marsalis likes to let the audience know that he is one of them. For example, in the summer of 1990 he did a concert in Brooklyn's Prospect Park—not far from where he was living at the time. That same night the Mets were playing on the west coast. The game would be starting at 10:30 P.M. New York time.

When he finished his program, Marsalis announced that he would love to stay and play all night. But he said, if he hurried back to his house, he could catch almost all of the game on television. The home-town crowd, loaded with Mets fans, laughed and applauded—and let him go after a short encore.

In early 1991 pianist Kenny Kirkland decided to

In the summer of 1990, Marsalis and his "crazy people" quartet performed in Brooklyn's Prospect Park, near where he lived. After a brief encore, he hurried home to watch a Mets game on television.

leave the quartet. Kirkland and Marsalis had been musical comrades for nearly ten years. They played together in the first Wynton Marsalis quintet, and were fired together when they joined Sting's "Blue Turtles" band. Kirkland appeared on five of Marsalis' first six albums as well as the *Mo' Better Blues* soundtrack.

"I couldn't find any pianists out there who could replace Kenny," Marsalis lamented.[10] So he didn't replace him. The Branford Marsalis quartet simply became the Branford Marsalis trio. The saxophonist continued working with just Hurst and Watts, bass and drums, but without piano.

Many jazz critics—and even some musicians—believe that working in a pianoless group poses special and frightening challenges for a soloist. The piano supplies the harmonic structure—often called the "chord changes"—of the song as the soloist improvises. Without the harmonic life raft, it is thought, the improviser may feel adrift, lost in a turbulent sea of music.

Marsalis, however, disagrees with that notion. "It's really strange to me," he said in a 1992 *Down Beat* interview, "that whenever you say trio, people say, 'man, you must've been terrified.'" Too many musicians, he maintains, "hang on to that piano for dear life." Marsalis, on the other hand, adapted to the pianoless setting quite easily.

"I used to sing to myself," he continued. ". . . I've always known if I could sing the song in my head, I could play the melody on my horn." The idea, Marsalis feels, is to be able to *hear* the piano part in your mind as you are playing the written melody—or improvising an original one—on your instrument. "If I can do that," he concluded, pointing to his head, "then the piano's right here."[11]

Marsalis first put that theory into practice on his 1989 album *Trio Jeepy*, recorded with just bass and drums. He did it again on his September 1991 release, *The Beautyful Ones Are Not Yet Born*. The earlier session has a loose, jam-session atmosphere, and Marsalis admitted that he was disappointed with it. The new recording, however, displays the unity and collective confidence of a real working band.

In a five-star review, *Down Beat*'s Bill Milkowski declared that *The Beautyful Ones Are Not Yet Born* is an "adventurous, excellent album . . . easily his best." He praised its "extraordinary moments of interplay and group improvisation" and marveled how Marsalis, Hurst, and Watts "seem to be breathing the music together."[12]

On one track the trio is joined by saxophonist Courtney Pine, an emerging jazz talent from London, England. On another Wynton Marsalis makes his first recorded appearance under his brother's leadership. The song's title, "Cain & Abel"—named for the two feuding brothers in the Bible—illustrates both Branford's devilish sense of humor and the fact that he and Wynton are able to laugh about their disagreements.

One Sunday morning that September, just days before the new album came out, Marsalis flew into New York's JFK Airport, having completed a grueling tour of Great Britain. He would have a three-day break before beginning a five-night, sold-out engagement at New York City's Joyce Theater, celebrating the release of *The Beautyful Ones Are Not Yet Born*.

It was an awfully busy three days off. His first night back Marsalis—jet lag and all—joined Sting in concert. On Monday he really did take a break. Marsalis sat in his season box at Shea Stadium, watching the Mets wind down another frustrating season.

Tuesday night he stopped by Madison Square Garden to sit in with the Grateful Dead. Afterward he headed down to a Greenwich Village nightclub to hear jazz pianist McCoy Tyner. "All kinds of music in the world," Marsalis mused.[13]

On Wednesday morning he was back to work. Marsalis woke up early to tape a segment for one of the morning television shows. He had gotten about four hours of sleep. Later that day he met his friend, pop pianist Bruce Hornsby, for some one-on-one basketball. By evening he was ready to open at the Joyce.

The audiences were an odd and unusual mix, especially for a jazz concert—blacks, whites, Asians, Latinos, jazz lovers, Sting fans, hip-hoppers,

Dead-heads—demonstrating Marsalis' broad appeal. Someone called out that he had seen Marsalis on Tuesday with the Grateful Dead. "Well," the saxophonist responded, "let's see if you like *this*."[14] Just about everyone did.

Jazz critic Jeff Levenson, reporting on the Joyce Theater engagement, paints a vivid picture of how the members of the trio work together, welding their separate contributions into a single musical structure. "[Watts] served as the percussion architect," he wrote, "building free-floating edifices of rhythm that Marsalis and his saxophone dressed with tuneful melodies. . . . Hurst, the good-soldiered mediator, tethered this sonic construction, and kept it from floating out of the building."[15]

On their final night Branford's father, Ellis Marsalis, who just finished a performance of his own at Carnegie Hall, stopped by to sit in. It was a happy reunion, personally and professionally.

After the show Marsalis, having done seven concerts in eight days, was tired. He thought about going home and getting some rest. Then he remembered that one of his favorite saxophonists, Joe Henderson, was playing at a club in the Village. He could rest tomorrow.

And Marsalis had better rest tomorrow. In four days he would be taking off for another month on the road. Being a professional jazz musician is one hectic way to make a living. But Marsalis is somehow grateful for it all.

"I live a charmed life," he has said, philosophically. ". . . If it wasn't for jazz and the conception of what jazz demands from a musician, . . . I would be like any other pop saxophone player."[16] So if being on the road for three hundred days a year is what Branford Marsalis needed to become a better musician, then maybe it was worth it.

"Everything"

As the fall of 1991 approached, all of show business was buzzing over one of the biggest stories in years—after almost three decades behind NBC's late-night desk, Johnny Carson was quitting *The Tonight Show.* Carson's long-time musical director and comic foil, the flamboyant trumpeter Doc Severinsen, also was leaving the program.

With Carson as its host, *The Tonight Show* grew into a television institution. By the early 1990s, however, its ratings started to slip. Carson's comedy bits and Severinsen's 1940s-style big band music seemed old-fashioned to the younger, hipper television viewers. They began tuning in to other late-night shows, such as the one hosted by the younger, hipper Arsenio Hall.

So NBC named Jay Leno, a comedian with a much

younger appeal, as Carson's replacement. But who would take Severinsen's place? Many musicians wanted the lucrative, high-profile gig. By early October Helen Kushnick, who was then the program's new executive producer, was swamped with résumés and audition tapes. She asked Bobby Colomby, senior vice-president of creative development for Sony, to help her narrow down the choices.

Kushnick sent him boxes of tapes and résumés, but Colomby already had an idea of his own. He recommended Branford Marsalis. (Marsalis records for Columbia, whose parent company is Sony—Colomby's employer.) Kushnick liked the idea and contacted the saxophonist.

He was reluctant at first, but agreed to meet with Leno. They got along so well—and Marsalis had grown so weary of his road schedule—that when NBC offered him the position, he accepted.

Marsalis jumped right in. He composed a more contemporary-sounding theme song for the revamped program. He also assembled a smaller, more adaptable *Tonight Show* band, starting with his favorite rhythm section—Kenny Kirkland, Robert Hurst, and Jeff "Tain" Watts. To fill out the group, Marsalis brought trombonist Matt Finders and guitarist Kevin Eubanks from New York, and added two west coast players—trumpeter Sal Marquez and percussionist Vicki

Randall. (Randall is the first woman musician ever to perform regularly with *The Tonight Show* band.)

This was not going to be, strictly speaking, a "jazz gig." Marsalis' band would have to play all kinds of music and only some of it would be jazz. Still, Kenny Kirkland was excited about his new job. "It's great that I'm part of this opportunity to play jazz in people's houses all over the country."[1]

And due largely to Marsalis' influence, the amount of jazz on *The Tonight Show* has greatly increased. Top jazz acts such as the Modern Jazz Quartet, tenor saxophonist Joe Henderson, pianist Eddie Palmieri and his Latin jazz band, and bassist Charlie Haden's Quartet West have been guests on the show.

Marsalis also has invited such outstanding jazz players as alto saxophonist Bobby Watson, trombonists Robin Eubanks and Steve Turre, clarinetist Don Byron, and pianists Geri Allen and James Williams to sit in with his band. Performing for between five and eight million television viewers is a rare opportunity for jazz artists, and the exposure can give them an important boost.

"After my appearance," Geri Allen recalls, "I got feedback from all over the country. . . . People were suddenly aware of me in a different kind of way." As a result, Allen reports that sales of her current recording increased.[2]

Just before he joined *The Tonight Show,* Marsalis returned to his first saxophone—the alto. He had put

Branford Marsalis and *The Tonight Show* band—left to right: trumpeter Sal Marquez, Marsalis, trombonist Matt Finders, bassist Robert Hurst, drummer Jeff "Tain" Watts, guitarist Kevin Eubanks, percussionist Vicki Randall, and pianist Kenny Kirkland.

the instrument aside more than ten years earlier when he switched to the tenor saxophone with Wynton's band. Marsalis's alto, along with his usual tenor and soprano saxes, can be heard on his 1992 release, a blues-oriented project titled *I Heard You Twice the First Time.*

The album is a change of pace for Marsalis, setting original jazz compositions in his freewheeling, "crazy people" style alongside more traditional blues songs. He performs in a variety of settings—trio, quartet, sextet—and is joined by renowned blues singers John Lee Hooker, Linda Hopkins, and B. B. King. Wynton Marsalis also appears on one track.

I Heard You Twice the First Time was met with solid reviews in the leading jazz publications. *Down Beat* found the album "stirring, [and] sincere," and noted that "the saxophonist mixes well with the guests on the three vocal cuts."[3] *Jazz Times* observed that "Branford Marsalis' recordings continue to be unpredictable, [and] full of chancetaking," and recommended "this thought-provoking set" to its readers.[4]

The album earned Marsalis his eighth Grammy nomination—in the category, "Best Jazz Instrumental Performance, Individual or Group"—and his first Grammy award. Then in 1994, Marsalis and pianist Bruce Hornsby shared the "Best Pop Instrumental" Grammy for Hornsby's single, "Barcelona Mona."

Ever since his scene-stealing appearance in the 1985 Sting documentary, *Bring on the Night,* Marsalis seemed

90

ripe for his own film showcase. In June 1992, *The Music Tells You*—an hour-long, behind-the-scenes portrait of Marsalis by documentary filmmakers D. A. Pennebaker and Chris Hegedus—premiered during New York's annual JVC Jazz Festival.

The film follows Marsalis through a variety of settings—in a recording studio, on stage with both his trio and Sting's group, backstage at Madison Square Garden with Jerry Garcia of the Grateful Dead, conducting a music clinic at Indiana University, and of course, on the road. Janet Maslin, *The New York Times*'s film critic, praised its "simple, penetrating style" and remarked that "Mr. Marsalis is revealed as an uncommonly articulate musician with distinct ideas about his work in particular and jazz in general."[5]

The documentary also provides a vivid look at the pleasures and frustrations of the saxophonist's pre-*Tonight Show* life as a traveling jazz musician. At one point, just before taking the stage, a weary Marsalis sighs, "I don't feel like it tonight. . . . I feel like a day off." Still he does go on, and performs brilliantly. The long musical sequence that follows illustrates the remarkable level of interaction and collective creativity that propels the trio through its live performances.

There is no doubt that Marsalis is glad to be off the road. Still his schedule as *The Tonight Show*'s musical director keeps him busy enough. "Everybody thinks this is an easy gig," he reflects. "And as far as the gig goes, it is easy. But what I have to do . . . "[6]

Most mornings Marsalis works out at the gym before arriving at the NBC studio around 1:00 P.M. However he often has to come in early to do an interview. He spends the afternoon composing and arranging music for the show, meeting with Leno and the program's staff, rehearsing with the band and that night's musical guests, and perhaps, even taping a short comedy segment.

The program is taped at between 5:30 P.M. and 6:30 P.M., but when the closing credits have finished rolling, Marsalis' day may be far from over. He sometimes will stay at the studio until the early morning hours, preparing for the next night's show. "So when you think about the gig," he emphasizes, "the gig is not just that hour that people see."[7]

The Tonight Show is something very rare for jazz musicians—a steady, high-visibility, well-paying job. However most of their playing takes place during commercial breaks, which can become very frustrating. As drummer Jeff "Tain" Watts notes, "You don't get to stretch out."[8]

To satisfy their need to "stretch out," Marsalis and the others perform frequently in jazz clubs around Los Angeles. "Now we don't have to worry about making money," he comments, "so we can play in these one-hundred-seat clubs just for the hell of it."[9]

During weeks when *The Tonight Show* is on

hiatus—the television industry's word for "reruns"—Marsalis still may go out for brief engagements in nightclubs or concert halls around the United States. But he is just as likely to head back to New York City and his favorite leisure-time activities. "Go to some Knick games," he says. "Chill with my son."[10]

Meanwhile, Marsalis just keeps acquiring new projects. In January 1992 he became host of a weekly series for National Public Radio, *Jazzset*. The show features top jazz artists performing before live audiences at sites all over the world. During the spring of 1993, Marsalis hosted twelve episodes of NBC's long-running, weekly music program, *Friday Night Videos*. He also composed the soundtrack for an episode of the HBO horror series, *Tales from the Crypt* that aired in October 1993.

And another year meant another album. This time it was a hard-core, no-nonsense jazz date showcasing the trio of Marsalis, Robert Hurst, and Jeff "Tain" Watts. Recorded in concert at Indiana University in Bloomington, Indiana, the disc was simply titled, *Bloomington*.

Down Beat's reviewer Fred Bouchard called the album "cheerful, well-paced, and (above all) loose," and marveled at the saxophonist's energy and stamina. "He barely takes the horn out of his mouth for a solid hour," the critic observed.[11] *CD Review* named it "The Best Jazz CD of 1993." For his part Marsalis was extremely happy with *Bloomington,* "my best and most adventurous album to date," he declared.[12]

But he was already looking ahead to his next recording, a more pop-oriented project. "I'm working on an album that uses a lot of hip-hop beats and samples," Marsalis announced in mid-1993.[13] This spring 1994 release, titled *Buckshot LeFonque,* even includes two tracks with singer DJ Premier of the rap group Gang Starr.

"I've never done anything for more than five years," Marsalis once said.[14] And interestingly enough, he has a five-year contract with NBC. But however long he remains with *The Tonight Show,* Marsalis wants to spend time working with and inspiring young local musicians. "What I hope to do in Los Angeles," he says, "is to play in different parts of the city and get a whole bunch of high school kids to come down and start checking us out. I want to influence their playing and musicianship."[15]

But he feels he can be more than just a musical role model. Marsalis realizes that as America's most visible African-American musician he must shoulder a certain amount of responsibility. "If all of a sudden I'm gonna be thrust into the spotlight as a spokesman," he muses, "I'm gonna carry myself in a manner that I feel is exemplary. Some little black kid . . . , if he sees me talking and says, 'Wow, I want to talk like him,' I think that's great. I think I'll make a difference that way."[16]

So what does the future hold for Branford Marsalis?

"I'll be surprised if I'm playing music after I'm 40," he has predicted. He does not like the idea of being pigeonholed as "just" a musician, and so he rarely poses for publicity photos or magazine layouts with his instrument. "I have so many options open," Marsalis insists. "Teaching at school, making documentaries, writing a history of jazz, acting, maybe, there are so many things to do."[17]

Acting may be the most intriguing and most likely of these many options. But Marsalis knows that he must develop the natural talent he displayed in *Throw Momma From the Train* and *School Daze*. Even when he lived in New York City, he had an acting coach, and since moving to the west coast he has continued to study drama.

In 1991 Marsalis took another turn before the camera, appearing in a short film for the Showtime cable television channel as—of all things—a *trumpet* player! And in February 1994 he appeared in an episode of the NBC comedy series, *The Fresh Prince of Bel-Air*.

Although Marsalis is eager to do more acting, he realizes that it can be as time-consuming as playing the saxophone, and balancing the two might be difficult. "It's a mean horn," he has observed. "Put it down for a week, and you're in trouble."[18]

Once Marsalis was even offered the lead in a proposed television situation comedy. His manager, Anne Marie Wilkins, didn't think the project was right for him. "Branford," she asked, "what do you want to be?"

"I want to do one thing well," he told her.

"And what thing is that?" Wilkins wondered.

"Everything," he replied."[19]

So far in his brief but eventful career, everything that Branford Marsalis has tried, he *has* done well. What lies ahead, only he can tell—that is, if he knew himself. Of course legions of jazz fans hope that, no matter what else he does, Marsalis still will be making music when he is forty and fifty and sixty. But whatever road he decides to follow, the discipline that he developed playing jazz will serve him well.

Marsalis has been successful in three different musical fields—jazz, rock, and classical. He has earned renown as a recording artist, concert performer, bandleader, composer, television and radio personality, and film actor. He has done it all and remains the same easygoing guy from New Orleans. But after all, Branford Marsalis did not go chasing after fame. Maybe that's why it looks so good on him.

Chronology

1960—Born in Breaux Bridge, Louisiana, on August 26.

1967—Takes up the clarinet.

1975—Switches from clarinet to saxophone.

1978—Attends Southern University in Baton Rouge, Louisiana.

1979—Transfers to Berklee College of Music in Boston, Massachusetts.

1980—Tours Europe with Art Blakey's big band in summer; during Christmas break, works two-week gig with Lionel Hampton's big band.

1981—Leaves Berklee to join Clark Terry's big band; later works with Art Blakey's Jazz Messengers and the Wynton Marsalis quintet.

1983—Makes worldwide tour with Herbie Hancock's VSOP II quintet.

1984—Releases debut recording as a leader, *Scenes in the City;* begins performing with his own quartet; records with Miles Davis.

1985—Makes final appearance with Wynton Marsalis' quintet; tours and records with rock singer-musician Sting.

1986—Releases second jazz album, *Royal Garden Blues,* and classical album, *Romances for Saxophone.*

1987—Has supporting role in feature film, *Throw Momma From the Train; Renaissance* released.

1988—Tours with Sting; appears in Spike Lee film, *School Daze; Random Abstract* released.

1989—Performs with Sonny Rollins at Carnegie Hall; *Trio Jeepy* released; forms working quartet with Kenny Kirkland, Robert Hurst, and Jeff "Tain" Watts.

1990—New release, *Crazy People Music,* signals a new, mature style; composes and records music for Spike Lee's *Mo' Better Blues;* performs on soundtrack of *The Russia House.*

1991—Spends almost three hundred days on the road for second consecutive year; trio album, *The Beautyful Ones Are Not Yet Born,* released.

1992—Takes over as musical director of *The Tonight Show;* is subject of documentary film, *The Music Tells You;* blues-oriented album, *I Heard You Twice the First Time,* released.

1993—Wins first Grammy Award, after seven nominations; hosts *Friday Night Videos;* tenth jazz album, *Bloomington,* released.

1994—Wins second Grammy Award; appears on *The Fresh Prince of Bel-Air; Buckshot LeFonque* released.

Selected Discography

As a Leader

Scenes in the City. (Columbia 38951, 1984.*)

Romances for Saxophone, with the English Chamber Orchestra. (Columbia 42122, 1986.)

Royal Garden Blues. (Columbia 40363, 1986.)

Renaissance. (Columbia 40711, 1987.)

Random Abstract. (Columbia 44055, 1988.)

Trio Jeepy. (Columbia 44199, 1989.)

Crazy People Music. (Columbia 46072, 1990.)

Music from "Mo' Better Blues." (Columbia 46792, 1990.)

The Beautyful Ones Are Not Yet Born. (Columbia 46990, 1991.)

I Heard You Twice the First Time. (Columbia 46083, 1992.)

Bloomington. (Columbia 52461, 1993.)

Buckshot LeFonque. (Columbia 57323, 1994)

* release date

With Other Artists

Art Blakey.
   Live at Montreux and North Sea. (Timeless 150.)
   Keystone 3. (Concord Jazz 196.)

Miles Davis.
   Decoy. (Columbia 38891.)

The Duke Ellington Orchestra.
Digital Duke. (GRP 1038.)

Dizzy Gillespie.
Closer to the Source. (Atlantic 81646.)
New Faces. (GRP 1012.)

The Grateful Dead.
Without a Net. (Arista 8634.)

Ellis and Wynton Marsalis.
Fathers and Sons. (Columbia 37972.)

Wynton Marsalis.
Wynton Marsalis. (Columbia 37574.)
Think of One. (Columbia 38641.)
Hot House Flowers. (Columbia 39530.)
Black Codes (From the Underground). (Columbia 40009.)

Sonny Rollins.
Falling in Love With Jazz. (Milestone 9179.)

Sting.
The Dream of the Blue Turtles. (A&M 3750.)
Bring on the Night. (A&M 6705.)
...Nothing Like the Sun. (A&M 6042.)
The Soul Cages. (A&M 6405.)

Tina Turner.
Break Every Rule. (Capitol 12530.)

Various Artists.
Do the Right Thing: Original Score. (Columbia 45406.)

Chapter Notes

Chapter 1

1. Michael Walker, "Late Night Sax," *Boston Globe Magazine*, September 7, 1992, p. 51.

2. Peter Watrous, "Here's Branford," *New York Times Magazine*, May 3, 1992, p. 40.

3. Josef Woodard, "The Revolution Might Be Televised," *Down Beat*, September 1992, p. 22.

4. Walker, p. 38.

5. Derek J. Caney, "It's a Tough Gig . . . ," *Windplayer*, vol. 9, no. 4, p. 6.

6. Woodard, p. 23.

7. Ibid.

8. Michael Bourne, "Heeeere's Branford," *Down Beat*, May 1992, p. 27.

9. Watrous, p. 72.

10. Ibid.

11. Walker, p. 51.

12. Gene Seymour, "A Difference in Pitch," *New York Newsday*, May 26, 1992, p. 43.

13. Woodard, p. 26.

14. Walker, p. 52.

Chapter 2

1. Thomas Sanction, "Horns of Plenty," *Time*, October 22, 1990, p. 67.

2. Eric Levin, "Branford Marsalis, Wynton's Big Brother, Blows His Own Horn in Jazz, Classics and Pop," *People*, January 18, 1986, p. 50.

3. A. James Liska, "Wynton and Branford Marsalis: A Common Understanding," *Down Beat*, December 1982, p. 15.

4. Levin, p. 49

5. Liska, p. 15

6. Eric Pooley, "Horn of Plenty," *New York,* October 14, 1991, p. 59.

7. Josef Woodard, "The Revolution Might Be Televised," *Down Beat,* September 1992, p. 24.

8. Clarence Weldon, "Branford Marsalis: Blowing His Own Horn," *Ebony,* February 1989, p. 70.

9. Kevin Whitehead, "The Many Sides of Branford Marsalis," *Down Beat,* March 1987, p. 18.

10. Levin, p. 53.

11. Stanley Crouch, "Wynton Marsalis: 1987," *Down Beat,* November, 1987, p. 18.

12. James Earl Hardy, "Ellis Marsalis: Father Jazz," *Essence,* June 1992, p. 51.

13. Wynton Marsalis, "Christmas Meant Football and Turkey—and a Swig o' Cranberry Bog," *TV Guide,* December 16, 1989, p. 12.

14. Ibid.

15. Delfeayo Marsalis, liner notes to Branford Marsalis: *The Beautyful Ones Are Not Yet Born,* Columbia 46990, 1991.

Chapter 3

1. Eric Pooley, "Horn of Plenty," *New York,* October 14, 1991, p. 59.

2. Kevin Whitehead, "The Many Sides of Branford Marsalis," *Down Beat,* March 1987, p. 18.

3. Eric Levin, "Branford Marsalis, Wynton's Big Brother, Blows His Own Horn in Jazz, Classics and Pop," *People,* November 18, 1988, p. 50.

4. Dimitri Ehrlich, "Marsalis and Pine," *Interview,* November 1990, p. 104.

5. Zan Stewart, "The Brash, Bright Branford Marsalis," *Los Angeles Times/Calendar,* November 25, 1990, p. 60.

6. Levin, p. 53.

7. Stewart, p. 60.

8. Michael Walker, "Late Night Sax," *Boston Globe Magazine*, September 7, 1992, p. 40.

9. Ibid.

10. Whitehead, p. 17.

11. Ibid., p. 18.

Chapter 4

1. Michael Segall, "The Romantic Marsalis," *Cosmopolitan*, October 1988, p. 62.

2. Peter Watrous, "Here's Branford," *New York Times Magazine*, May 3, 1992, p. 42.

3. Eric Pooley, "Horn of Plenty," *New York*, October 14, 1991, p. 60.

4. Ibid.

5. A. James Liska, "Wynton and Branford Marsalis: A Common Understanding," *Down Beat*, December 1982, p. 15.

6. Ibid., p. 16.

7. David Fricke, "The Two Worlds of Branford Marsalis," *Rolling Stone*, February 25, 1988, p. 16.

8. Michael Ullman, review of Branford Marsalis: *Scenes in the City*, *High Fidelity*, August 1984, p. 81.

9. J. B. Figi, review of Branford Marsalis: *Scenes in the City*, *Down Beat*, August 1984, p. 34.

10. Eric Levin, review of Branford Marsalis: *Scenes in the City*, *People*, April 23, 1988, p. 28.

11. Stuart Troup, "Tomorrow's Jazz Giants," *New York Newsday*, August 24, 1984, part II, p. 29.

12. Miles Davis (with Quincy Troupe), *Miles: The Autobiography* (New York: Simon and Schuster, 1989), p. 357.

13. Jeff Levenson, "Branford Marsalis: Self-Propelled Musical Dynamo," *Christian Science Monitor*, February 12, 1992, p. 14.

Chapter 5

1. Howard Mandel, "Branford Marsalis," *Down Beat*, August 1985, p. 14.

2. Zan Stewart, "The Brash, Bright Branford Marsalis," *Los Angeles Times/Calendar*, November 25, 1990, p. 6.

3. Kevin Whitehead, "The Many Sides of Branford Marsalis," *Down Beat*, March 1987, p. 17.

4. Michael Walker, "Late Night Sax," *Boston Globe Magazine*, June 7, 1992, p. 41.

5. Jim Miller, " 'Blue Turtles': Jazz Meets Rock," *Newsweek*, September 30, 1985, p. 69.

6. Victor Garbarini, "Bop to the Future," *Vogue*, November 1990, p. 260.

7. "Marsalis Still a Success With His New Jazz Band," *Jet*, September 1, 1986, p. 63.

8. Mandel, p. 14.

9. Eric Pooley, "Horn of Plenty," *New York*, October 14, 1991, p. 58.

10. Eric Levin, "Branford Marsalis, Wynton's Big Brother, Blows His Own Horn in Jazz, Classics and Pop," *People*, January 18, 1988, p. 50.

11. Ibid.

12. Peter Watrous, "Here's Branford," *New York Times Magazine*, May 3, 1992, p. 42.

13. Walker, p. 41.

14. Watrous, p. 42.

15. Levin, p. 53.

16. Watrous, p. 72.

17. Pooley, p. 60.

18. Stephen Fried, "The Holy Goof," *GQ,* May 1991, p. 203.

19. Ibid., p. 202.

20. Ibid., p. 203.

21. Ibid.

22. David Fricke, "The Two Worlds of Branford Marsalis," *Rolling Stone,* February 25, 1988, p 17.

23. Whitehead, p. 17.

24. William D. White, review of Sting: *Bring on the Night, Jazziz,* 1986.

25. Fricke, p. 16.

26. Pooley, p. 62.

Chapter 6

1. Clarence Weldon, "Branford Marsalis: Blowing His Own Horn," *Ebony,* February 1989, pp. 70–72.

2. Eric Levin, "Branford Marsalis, Wynton's Big Brother, Blows His Own Horn in Jazz, Classics and Pop," *People,* January 18, 1988, p. 50.

3. Cathleen McGuigan, "Branford's Two Worlds," *Newsweek,* January 4, 1988, p. 54.

4. Levin, p. 50.

5. Eric Pooley, "Horn of Plenty," *New York,* October 14, 1991, p. 61.

6. Geoffrey Himes, "Marsalis' Risk-Taking Sax," *Washington Post Weekend,* November 13, 1987, p. 22.

7. David Fricke, "The Two Worlds of Branford Marsalis," *Rolling Stone,* February 25, 1988, p. 17.

8. Bill Milkowski, "Gang of 2," *Down Beat,* January 1992, p. 19.

9. Chris Albertson, review of Branford Marsalis: *Random Abstract, Stereo Review,* November 1988, p. 130.

10. Clarence Weldon, "Branford Marsalis and Jay Leno Give 'Tonight Show' New Humor and New Sound," *Jet,* June 22, 1992, p. 58.

11. Jon Pareles, "It's Rollins vs. Marsalis in a Duel at Carnegie," *New York Times,* May 19, 1989, p. C20.

12. Jon Pareles, "Sonny Rollins' Twist on Calypso and Pop," *New York Times,* May 22, 1989, p. C12.

13. Greg Tate, "Jazz and the Family Stand," *Village Voice,* April 9, 1991, p. 67.

14. Milkowski, p. 19.

15. Art Lange, review of Branford Marsalis: *Trio Jeepy, Down Beat,* October 1989, p. 36.

16. Geoffrey Himes, "The Magical Marsalises," *Washington Post,* June 18, 1988, p. G12.

Chapter 7

1. Eric Pooley, "Horn of Plenty," *New York,* October 14, 1991, p. 61.

2. Ibid, p. 62.

3. Victor Garbarini, "Bop to the Future," *Vogue,* November 1990, p. 260.

4. Conrad Brunner, "New York Stories," *Straight, No Chaser,* Summer 1991, p. 27.

5. Zan Stewart, "The Brash, Bright Branford Marsalis," *Los Angeles Times/Calendar,* November 25, 1990, p. 59.

6. Chris Albertson, review of Branford Marsalis: *Crazy People Music* and *Mo' Better Blues,* original motion picture soundtrack, *Stereo Review,* November 1990, p. 155.

7. Stewart, pp. 6, 59.

8. Stephen Fried, "The Holy Goof," *GQ,* May 1991, p. 202.

9. Stewart, p. 59.

10. Peter Watrous, "Private Codes Enliven Jazz," *New York Times,* December 31, 1989, section 2, pp. 23–24.

Chapter 8

1. Zan Stewart, "The Brash, Bright Branford Marsalis," *Los Angeles Times/Calendar,* November 25, 1990, p. 60.

2. Ibid., p. 59.

3. Ibid.

4. Stephen Fried, "The Holy Goof," *GQ,* May 1991, p. 227.

5. Peter Watrous, "Here's Branford," *New York Times Magazine,* May 3, 1992, p. 72.

6. Eric Levin, "Branford Marsalis, Wynton's Big Brother, Blows His Own Horn in Jazz, Classics and Pop," *People,* January 18, 1988, p. 53.

7. Victor Garbarini, "Bop to the Future," *Vogue,* November 1990, p. 256.

8. Fried, p. 227.

9. Peter Watrous, "Branford Marsalis Band," *New York Times,* April 12, 1990, p. C16.

10. Peter Watrous, "The Pop Life," *New York Times,* October 16, 1991, p. C16.

11. Bill Milkowski, "Gang of 2," *Down Beat,* January 1992, p. 20.

12. Bill Milkowski, review of Branford Marsalis: *The Beautyful Ones Are Not Yet Born, Down Beat,* November 1991, pp. 35–36.

13. Eric Pooley, "Horn of Plenty," *New York,* October 14, 1991, p. 62.

14. Ibid, p. 58.

15. Jeff Levenson, "Branford Marsalis: Self-Propelled Musical Dynamo," *Christian Science Monitor,* February 12, 1992, p. 14.

16. Stewart, p. 6.

Chapter 9

1. Josef Woodard, "The Revolution Might Be Televised," *Down Beat,* September 1992, p. 23.

2. Fred Shuster, "The Reluctant Power Broker," *Down Beat,* July 1993, p. 17.

3. Owen Cordle, review of Branford Marsalis: *I Heard You Twice the First Time, Down Beat,* November 1992, p. 43.

4. Scott Yanow, review of Branford Marsalis: *I Heard You Twice the First Time, Jazz Times,* November 1992, pp. 64–65.

5. Janet Maslin, "On the Sax, Freedom Isn't Found in Freedom," *New York Times,* January 26, 1992, p. C12.

6. Don Heckman, "Branford," *Jazz Times,* June 1993, p. 25.

7. Ibid.

8. Woodard, p. 24

9. Ibid., p. 25.

10. Spike Lee, "Tonight, You'll Be Hearing Branford Marsalis," *Interview,* May 1992, p. 46.

11. Fred Bouchard, review of Branford Marsalis: *Bloomington, Down Beat,* July 1993, p. 45.

12. Shuster, p. 18.

13. Heckman, p. 96.

14. Clarence Weldon, "Branford Marsalis: Blowing His Own Horn," *Ebony,* February 1989, p. 70.

15. Woodard, p. 25.

16. Michael Walker, "Late Night Sax," *Boston Globe Magazine,* September 7, 1992, p. 52.

17. Peter Watrous, "Here's Branford," *New York Times Magazine,* May 3, 1992, p. 78.

18. Cathleen McGuigan, "Branford's Two Worlds," *Newsweek,* January 14, 1986, p. 54.

19. Eric Pooley, "Horn of Plenty," *New York,* October 14, 1991, p. 59.

Further Reading

Fried, Stephen. "The Holy Goof." *GQ,* May 1991.

Heckman, Don. "Branford." *Jazz Times,* June 1993.

Levin, Eric. "Branford Marsalis, Wynton's Big Brother, Blows His Own Horn in Jazz, Classics and Pop." *People,* January 18, 1988.

Liska, A. James. "Wynton and Branford Marsalis: A Common Understanding." *Down Beat,* December 1982. (Reprinted, September 1989; February 1994.)

Pooley, Eric. "Horn of Plenty." *New York,* October 14, 1991.

Shuster, Fred. "The Reluctant Power Broker." *Down Beat,* July 1993.

Stewart, Zan. "The Brash, Bright Branford Marsalis." *Los Angeles Times/Calendar,* November 25, 1990.

Walker, Michael. "Late Night Sax." *Boston Globe Magazine,* September 7, 1992.

Watrous, Peter. "Here's Branford." *New York Times Magazine,* May 3, 1992.

Weldon, Clarence. "Branford Marsalis: Blowing His Own Horn." *Ebony,* February 1989.

Whitehead, Kevin. "The Many Sides of Branford Marsalis." *Down Beat,* March 1987.

Woodard, Josef. "The Revolution Might Be Televised." *Down Beat,* September 1992.

Index

A

Allen, Geri, 88
Armstrong, Louis, 13

B

Batiste, Alvin, 20
Berklee College of Music, 20,
    21–22, 24, 26
big bands, 26–29
Blakey, Art, 23–24, 29, 31–34, 35
Blanchard, Terence, 68–69, 72
Butler, George, 78
Byron, Don, 88

C

Carter, Ron, 35, 41, 42, 53
Coleman, Ornette, 36
Colomby, Bobby, 87
Coltrane, John, 31, 36, 58, 66

D

Davis, Miles, 9, 37, 43–45, 46,
    47
DeVito, Danny, 56
Duke Ellington Orchestra, the,
    59

E

Ellington, Duke, 14, 34
Eubanks, Kevin, 87, 89
Eubanks, Robin, 42, 88

F

Felix, Delbert, 57, 60, 63
Finders, Matt, 29, 87, 89
Foster, Al, 53

G

Gang Starr, 54, 94

Garcia, Jerry, 68, 91
Grateful Dead, the, 8, 54,
    67–68, 83

H

Haden, Charlie, 88
Hakim, Omar, 47
Hampton, Lionel, 26–27, 29
Hancock, Herbie, 32, 35–36,
    41, 53, 67
Harrison, Donald, 22
Henderson, Joe, 84, 88
Hinton, Milt, 63–64
Hooker, John Lee, 90
Hopkins, Linda, 90
Hornsby, Bruce, 83, 90
Hurst, Robert, 36, 58, 60, 61,
    65, 70, 77–78, 81, 84,
    87, 89, 93

J

Jones, Daryl, 47
Jones, Elvin, 31

K

King, B.B., 61, 90
Kirkland, Kenny, 36, 39–40,
    42, 47–48, 51, 57, 58,
    60, 65, 69, 77–78,
    79–81, 87, 88, 89
Kushnick, Helen, 8, 87

L

Lee, Bill, 60, 68–69
Lee, Spike, 56–57, 60–62,
    68–70
Leno, Jay, 7–10, 86–87, 92

M

Marquez, Sal, 87, 89

Marsalis, Branford
  childhood, 15–20
  film and television
    appearances, 48, 54,
    56–57, 59, 68, 72–73,
    90–91, 93, 95
  Grammy nominations and
    awards, 8, 53, 59, 60, 64,
    72, 90
  life on the road, 9–11, 29–31,
    46–47, 74–78, 83–85, 91
  musical differences with
    Wynton Marsalis, 16–17,
    40–41, 48–50, 73, 82–83
  on being a role model, 94
  on differences between jazz
    and rock, 51–53
  on jazz, 17, 22–23, 66–67,
    81–82, 84–85
  on pop music, 16–17, 47,
    55, 83
  playing classical music, 20,
    47, 54
  practicing, 11, 15, 22,
    23–24, 52, 76, 95
  recordings as a leader, 99
    Bloomington, 93, 94
    Buckshot LeFonque, 94
    Crazy People Music,
      70–72
    *I Heard You Twice the
      First Time*, 90
    *Music from Mo' Better
      Blues*, 70–72
    Random Abstract, 59–60,
      70
    Renaissance, 57–58
    Romances for Saxophone,
      54
    Royal Garden Blues, 53, 57
    Scenes in the City, 42–43
    *The Beautyful Ones Are
      Not Yet Born*, 82–83
    Trio Jeepy, 63–64, 82
  recordings with other artists,
    24, 31, 34, 35–36,
    41–42, 43–45, 48, 54,
    63, 90, 99–100
  reviews of, 42–43, 48, 54,
    58, 60, 62, 64, 71, 73,
    82, 84, 90, 91, 93
  sense of humor, 30, 57,
    78–79, 82–83
  sports, 16, 21, 46–47, 57,
    67, 76, 83, 93
  Tonight Show, The, 7–12,
    74–75, 86–89, 91–93, 94
  working with other leaders,
    24, 29–42, 45–51, 54, 59

Marsalis, Delfeayo (brother),
  15, 17, 18, 50

Marsalis, Dolores (mother),
  14–15, 17–18

Marsalis, Ellis (father), 14,
  16–20, 31, 53, 84

Marsalis, Ellis III (brother), 18

Marsalis, Jason (brother), 15

Marsalis, Mboya (brother), 73

Marsalis, Reese (son), 11–12,
  51, 93

Marsalis, Wynton (brother), 8,
  15–20, 23–24, 31–32,
  34, 35–36, 38–42, 45,
  48–50, 73, 78, 82–83,
  90

Miller, Mulgrew, 42
Modern Jazz Quartet, the, 88
Moffett, Charnett, 42, 43

N
Nash, Lewis, 57, 60

P
Palmieri, Eddie, 88
Parker, Charlie, 22–23
Pine, Courtney, 82
Public Enemy, 54

R
Randall, Vicki, 87–88, 89
Reese, Teresa (ex-wife), 11, 47
Rollins, Sonny, 58, 62–63, 66

S
Sanborn, David, 8–9, 17
Shorter, Wayne, 31, 58, 66
Smith, Marvin "Smitty," 22, 42, 43
Snipes, Wesley, 68
Sting, 8, 47–55, 59, 63, 67, 91

T
Taylor, Cecil, 37
Terry, Clark, 26, 29–31
Turner, Tina, 54
Turre, Steve, 88
Tyner, McCoy, 83

W
Washington, Jr., Grover, 17
Watson, Bobby, 88
Watts, Jeff "Tain," 22, 36, 42, 60, 61, 63–64, 65, 69, 70, 77–78, 81, 84, 87, 89, 92, 93
Webster, Ben, 58
Wilkins, Anne Marie, 95
Williams, James, 88
Williams, Tony, 35, 41, 53, 58
Willis, Larry, 43

Y
"Young Lions" movement in jazz, 8, 36–39, 78